21st Century United States of America:

Land of the Free, Home of the Homeless

By Katie Day

Kind of a memoir- with an overarching awareness objective

Minneapolis, MN, USA ~ 2012

21st Century United States of America: Land of the Free, Home of the Homeless

ISBN: 978-0-615-67233-5

Spiritual Guide and Life Coach: Stannie Hinn the Lhasa Apso (pictured above)

Edited and Cover Design by Katie Day

Publisher: Stannie Hinn Enterprises

Printed by Lulu

For more information or to order copies contact the author at daykatie@hotmail.com

Dedicated to everyone living in

the conditions of poverty

From Section I of the 13th Amendment to the United States Constitution:

Neither slavery nor involuntary servitude, except as a punishment for crime whereof the party shall have been duly convicted, shall exist within the United States, or any place subject to their jurisdiction.

The song title and acknowledgement of a particular artist's version for each chapter occurred happenstance. I love all types of music, and when I hear a song I like- I usually stumble onto the various versions of it performed (and locate the original). It depends on my mood as to which one captures my fancy on a particular day- part of the fun is the hunt!

"Sitting Here in Limbo" was an unintended seed that structured the whole format of this book. A writing bug bit me while listening to it one day. I have no formal writing education outside of reading books and what I did for school and work- so I have no apologies for run on sentences, misuse of commas--- or too many dashes. And have discovered that proof reading, copyediting, and formatting a book into paperback format is more difficult than the actual writing itself (maybe, maybe not- I have dreamed of having these services provided for me a million times during the process... but the amount of money being saved is priceless).

I proceeded with the other 3 observational story essays (respectively; Let Me Lie, Fast Train, and Mohammed's Radio)- completed them in about 3 months and put them away. I then just wrote and wrote for over a year. Positively 4th Street, Said What You Mean, For the Good Times, and Hobo Jungle are consolidated argumentative essays that have been tweaked and revised for the past year and a half.

This play list of songs is a mere morsel of the catalog of 'writing bug' inducing songs (and artists) I rely on, but these best captured each essay's sentiment (in the moment I chose them anyway). If I were to 'pick' an album to convey the whole mood of the book – maybe it would be Yankee Hotel Foxtrot by Wilco. Who knows? I wouldn't have 'discovered' many of these great tunes and artists without getting inoculated with during high school- and obsessed with while in college- one of my hometown faves, The Big Wu.

Contents

Me and Gramma (undergrad Commencement- 2002)

Acknowledgements

I feel arrogant writing for an audience beyond my friends and family, but here it goes. My parents are both full time hard working people that provided a childhood full of so many opportunities and fun. I am in awe. There were three of us kids chasing each other around the house, cracking our skulls and severing our toes, as we 'played' all summer long. We always called and let them know about any mishaps- and to ask permission for things like what to eat for lunch and turning on the air conditioner. I am the youngest, and would call to tattle on either of them for doing just about anything. That is, when I wasn't throwing roller skates against bedroom doors or kicking the T.V. off its stand (I got frustrated playing Kung Ku on Nintendo, and took it a bit too far one day).

They obviously did 'something' right- because I am pretty mellow and don't watch much T.V. (although I am a complete Wire junkie). And for the most part, I have incredible relationships with my brother and sister. The 'majority' of my parent's free time was spent coaching and shuttling us to various organized sports- and revolving weekends around all our meets and tournaments. I swam competitively (which means on a private club that cost money, I wasn't that fast, but I love to swim) from age 6 to 14. Their philosophy was

8

for us to 'try' every sport until we picked the ones we liked. I tried dance and soccer- but ended up sticking with swimming, softball and basketball (I'm glad my dad coached many of the 'traveling' teams, because I was 'good'- but not 'traveling' team caliber).

We have a family cabin that I spent as much time as I could in the summer while growing up. The teacher schedule that my cabin buddy's mom had was great, because sometimes I was lucky enough to spend a week with them while my family went back to the city. I also went to Y.M.C.A., Girl Scout, and horse camps. And traveled with the church hand bell choir to festivals across the country (and Canada!). Sometimes I just have to stop and remember how blessed I am. Thanks mom and dad. And to learn that my dad was unemployed for a few of those years amazes me even more- we had no clue – or at least I didn't.

Chapter One

Positively 4th Street
As performed by Bob Dylan

I first remember 'considering' socioeconomic conditions after a basketball game in 6th or 7th grade. One of my 'fans' came up to me and observed:

"Gee Katie, those blacks are such good athletes, I can't believe you guys don't any on your team"

I thought about it and replied

"Yes, they are great athletes, but it costs a lot of money to play on these teams- and a lot of them don't have enough money to do it"

"Boy Katie, I never thought about it like that, you are right, well isn't that a shame…"

I realize that this person already thought about it like that; and was providing me with a gift- a gift to think for myself. She rewarded me with a bit of intellectual confidence by pretending I 'taught' her something. I know for certain at age 32- that any of my 'understandings' at age 11 or 12 were constructions of what I was surrounded by- and that anyone who had lived more than my adolescent years on this earth already 'knew' about the unjust socioeconomic conditions that plague this world.

I find the most evolutionary truth in this exchange is how my understanding had absolutely nothing to do with biology (aside from the application of general skin tone racial designations)- just money. My response carried no hint of the negative understandings or beliefs of biological inferiority that was once used as justification to enslave people and their cultures.

I grew up being taught the value in treating other people the way you want to be treated. I considered the increased usage of reduced lunches and inability to pay for expensive extra curricular activities, among my non-white friends and classmates, to be a matter of random circumstance- not a consequence of historical policies rooted in the belief that they were an inferior class of people. The suburban 'middle' class school system I attended was not overtly racist, but its economic and social patterns were shaped by our country's longstanding color line.

I eventually realized that the way I once viewed race and income was flawed. My young understanding was silent and innocent, but embraced a subtle logic that somehow linked poverty to communities of color- without any type of historical basis. It was as 'simple' as declaring the sky is blue or the sun is yellow. It was a reflection of what I saw and absorbed in our culture, and not connected to any ideas of inferiority or superiority. But it was an understanding that most certainly didn't ask the question "why?"

As a kid (and teenager) I did a lot of fun things- and a lot of stupid things. I think everyone can accept most playground and childhood memories as indispensable. I am lucky that the majority of mine are filled with love and adventure, but I have a 'few' that rattle my core.

Things I wish I didn't do, but I did. Like 'jokingly' asking my parents "What color is my skin?" when told to fetch them something- that did not receive a warm response and was quickly retired from my repertoire. Or how I considered the 'threat' posed to me by the neo Nazi literature given to me by some of my 7th grade classmates. I never did more than read and ponder the piece of paper; and I remember asking my brother if the projected non-white majority of U.S. citizens in 2050 was a 'concern' worth worrying about. Needless to say, I didn't join the group and I distanced myself from the kids getting involved in it.

One of my girlfriends has two 'redneck'... or, a couple of brothers who prefer living in the country as opposed to the city. She shared with me the 'naughty' lyric improvisation one of them made to Tim McGraw's chart topping "Don't Take the Girl." Instead of "...stranger came and pulled a gun" he improvised with "Nigger came and pulled a gun." We were more intrigued by the 'shock' value than the racial overtone. Or I think we were- I remember talking about it with her, but we never sang them out loud or identified any allegiance to them.

I question whether I should consider these recollections fortunate or unfortunate, because again, childhood memories are indispensible. And mine seem to reflect the more curious, rather than disruptive, person that I am. I had an upbringing removed from any struggle, which most likely influences the way I interact with people. I had no fear or stress in regards to meeting my basic needs. Thus, no 'need' (or reason) for me to identify with people or behaviors to fulfill any emotional or physical needs not being met at home.

These memories do, however, show how susceptible and vulnerable our human thoughts and actions are to the environments around us.

I don't begrudge the kid for teaching me the "what color is my skin" joke, and the respect I hold for my friend and her brothers is not diminished- her brothers were 'kids' too, and they never acted out beyond producing inappropriate lyric improvisations. Soon after being introduced to that lyric, I began dating a 'black' guy. The same 'boys' that wanted me to join their club, just two years earlier, were now angrily chasing me down our high school hallways. And when they finally had me cornered- they verbally assaulted me while kicking my shins and spitting in my face... for being a 'traitor' and 'nigger' lover.

My brother and his buddies prevented any similar attacks from happening to me. Not sure how it went down, but I think the ratio between the quantity and physical size of athletes, from various races, in my brother's crew compared to the neo Nazi crew was the actual weapon. I do know that there were no broken bones or missing body parts... and that I was forever changed. I had gotten my first dose of 'overt' racism- and was on the receiving end of an emotional power capable of evoking hatred in some of its willing practitioners.

From there, my remaining teenage years were filled with locating the next 'best' social gathering and inducting myself permanently into working class society. I got my first job at age 12 delivering a weekly suburban paper. I ventured into bagging groceries, slicing bagels, serving up soft serve ice cream cones, and sorting out other people's dry cleaning garments; before finding the 'bread and butter' occupation that would get me through college. During my junior year of high school, our family's exchange student from Russia hooked me up with a job at Applebee's.

Being a restaurant server was a primer for me to begin understanding the socioeconomic spectrum. And by 'socioeconomic', I am referring to the overall economic, social, and political positions people hold in society. The 'spectrum' relates to the historically ingrained positions people are born into- because of the socially constructed class structure initially designed (and implemented by government) to designate people into an economic caste labor system based on their race. And the 'conditions' refer to the modern day living realities of the spectrum. Socioeconomics camouflages the discourse and framework on how our country's racist past is still living today- and I will expand on that assertion later. Back to the restaurant experience...

The clientele is where the 'majority' of U.S. citizens rank on the spectrum. Using a scale that designates the lowest economic, social, and political position below the deepest 'poverty' level and the highest position above Warren Buffet and Bill Gates territory. The people that can regularly frequent all American restaurants rank in the middle- although the household income range in this segment greatly varies- they dine out because they can either afford to sneak in quick sit down lunch breaks from work or fill their bellies with $12 salads 'just because'...

Those of us who serve and prepare the food and drinks encompass positions in the middle to 'lower' end of spectrum. And I must say, the non-white populations I worked with colored both my world and work experiences. I am still astounded by the pleasant greetings I always received from many Latino hosts, hostesses, cooks, dishwashers, and food preparers- no matter how busy or chaotic the moment was. And to realize that this job was only one of the two or three they held at all times. It was these 'back of house' restaurant operations where I began to realize how concrete and embedded the socioeconomic spectrum is in our society.

My high school academic ambitions were zero. The education conversations I had with my parents had little to do with academics, and more to do with the

16

trouble I got in- but I somehow managed to maintain an above C average (a steep decline from my elementary and middle school level averages). The trouble I got into wasn't horrendous. Skipping classes here, engaging in some underage drinking there- and basically not focusing or caring about being educated.

I headed off with a bunch of friends to attend community college in the warm sun of Arizona. A no brainer because I had easy access to the college trust fund my grandparents set up. Heck, I had been going to school and working a serving job for the last two years of high school- why not continue that great lifestyle while being away from parents and surrounded by friends? With swimming pools around every corner to cool off from the forever summer weather!

I knew I could financially 'handle' it. Or, I thought I could since I had saved up enough to buy myself a used car, and figured any money that I would have saved could now go towards rent and food. I had to make some serious adjustments in relation to keeping toilet paper stocked, etc... (And received some help from my parents), but I did it! More importantly, I rediscovered my own curiosity and love for learning... all because, as an adult, I know that I am not down with injustice- of any kind.

"Please step out into the hall if you missed the test last week" announced my Communications professor. I turned to my classmate and earnestly asked, "We took a test?"

The consequence for disregarding that test was that I had to enter a speech competition to make up enough extra credit to pass the class. I was not a fan of public speaking and began aimlessly meandering around campus wondering why I was even in college in the first place. But those wonders disappeared when I arrived late to my Sociology class. The class topic was on racial profiling, and the elusive detriment of this phenomenon enraptured me. I chose the topic for my speech.

As I gathered information, I began realizing how complex and invigorating racism is in our country. I ended up receiving a trophy for second place in the competition. The significance of this academic accomplishment is evident in the rest of my undergrad performance. I was suddenly engaged and actually trying. Despite withdrawing from 7 or 8 classes during the first 2.5 years of undergrad, I vivaciously earned a Bachelor's degree within 4.5 years. Not too shabby for someone who entered the world of higher education with little interest and no ambition.

I could not believe that racism existed. Sounds ridiculous, right? I'm serious. The racial profiling example in class was about the scientific proof revealing how mall clerks and other retailers literally stalk people who look 'poor' … to make sure they don't steal. Or, the shopping experience for people with a darker skin tone is different than that of their white counterparts.

Remember how I described my 'childhood' understanding of poverty and people from communities of color? Well I had no idea that an alarming rate of white people with (or managing) money conducted themselves in such a disruptive manner. This changed everything. Especially since, I myself, benefited from such discrimination. Or, as a 'teen' I happily accompanied my friends to the shopping mall to point out 'things' that I wouldn't steal myself, but had no problem accepting after they took the risk.

How crazy is that? My white girlfriends and I had (and still have) a better chance of fleecing retail stores simply because of the public perception and industry practice to hone in on non-white people- who have no more of a predisposition to steal than any white people- no one comes out of the womb stealing.

Now I only went on one or two of those fleecing expeditions, and I have no idea what the sum of our thieving was, but the motivation was for the thrill more than the need. I think some jewelry from Claire's and overpriced Giraud's were the most expensive items. After all, we had to hide the 'contraband' from our parents.   Not cool or proud of it; but the combination of that contradiction and the degree of hostility, directed towards me for simply dating a black guy, solidified my desire to begin channeling my energy into understanding how something so wrong carries on as if it is right. And how had I been so unaware of it?

I wanted to understand the historical context of this epidemic so that I could constructively contribute to it in the present. To do this, I enrolled in a Bachelor's of Arts in Ethnic Studies program at Metropolitan State University. Boy, the 'problem' extended way beyond aggressive stalking by retail clerks in suburban shopping malls.

And wow, school is quite enjoyable when you become engaged in the challenge. I had (and still have) so much to learn, but I knew that simply declaring a stance against injustice is not conducive to doing anything meaningful about it. It was time for me to learn more about injustice from people who have more insight on being on the receiving end of it.

The faculty of the Ethnic Studies department was all non-white. The premise of the degree program is to provide an economic, social, and political history of the United States through a non-white perspective. Most of my fellow Ethnic Studies cohort was either non-white or older than myself. The school caters to 'working' higher education seekers. It was a small program, both in terms of the amount of faculty and students, with class sizes ranging from 10 to 30 students. The curriculum and classroom discussions were bar none; the most intellectually invigorating, honest and respectfully uncomfortable I have ever been a part of. I was far away from the typical college experience that many of my white friends were experiencing- and I loved it. For the first time in my life, I felt like I was involved in something more than going through the motions and figuring out the next best social gathering.

As an aside, I was also taking on more responsibility in my own life. Or, I no longer needed the $300 a month rental subsidy that my parents sent me throughout my time in Arizona. I was paying my own (higher) rent and living on a budget based on my income. I was no longer selfishly quitting jobs by faking appendix ruptures or telling bosses other obscure lies when their scheduling needs didn't fit my social calendar.

While there were only a handful of professors, and all of them were great, two really took the time to help me along. One must understand how ignorant I was in relation to all these brilliant professors and students. I couldn't even identify my ancestral lineage during the 'introduce yourself' exercise in the "Introduction to Theories About Race and Ethnicity in the United States" class- let alone properly appreciate the pervasiveness of socioeconomic conditions in our country.

Not that it 'matters'- but the two extra helpful professors were both American Indian. How did they help me along? Well both of them met with me outside of class to read and go over my 50-page capstone, which helped build my confidence- and changed the way I thought of myself because I now had something of 'value' to offer. Seriously, what does our society value? Fame and fortune— I had stunted my academic 'progress' before college, and never aspired for fame or fortune- so before, I was literally 'coasting' along in society. Just another average white female face that is so objectified and heavily advertised to in society. So they 'indirectly' helped me reevaluate my own value of myself.

They were also approachable to the shy trust fund white do gooder student that had no idea how to contribute to the long and erroneous challenge of dismantling systemic racism. My academic 'chops' were rough; so I was, as one them delicately phrased, "a spatial rather than linear" thinker. The other one was a little more direct; and told me that I had potential to go further in school, but needed to "get your shit together because graduate school professors will have no mercy on you being unprepared." The most critical revelation I learned from this degree is that communities of color can determine their own measures to meet their own means in achieving economic stability, and that I must honor this fact while constructing my own role.

I wanted to understand poverty- and see how it is systemically 'managed'- so I could help change it. The textbook knowledge I gained would be useless without hands on experience... but there were not a lot of jobs 'available' fitting that description. So after graduation, I plunged into the trenches as a childcare worker and transitioned into various case and program management positions in the non-profit 'human service' sector. I was employed by three different agencies over the course of 8 years. I was continually inspired by the hard fought battles people make everyday in achieving stability. To actually see a person ascend from a difficult road of despair to a more stable road on higher ground is what will keep me there until a more even path is built for everyone.

The rewards for these ascensions do not match the perseverance demonstrated by the people facing multiple obstacles. We are born into positions on the socioeconomic spectrum that places us relation to poverty- and the overrepresentation of non-white populations living in poverty casts a dark shadow on the individual inspiring triumphs. As well as the inclusion of white people- I do not 'favor' one race's circumstance over another.

We are now entering a new era where people are not only living in the conditions of poverty, but they are also being systemically classified as 'homeless'- our country now considers homelessness to be a segment of our 'society.' As if poverty is now a condition that we expect people to live with instead of being subject to living in AND moving out of- it's as if we've thrown the 'bootstrap' theory (which had no real teeth anyway) out with the kitchen sink. It is, to paraphrase someone near a dear to me, "a shame."

The following four chapters are essays I began writing a year and a half prior to this one. It was during a time when I had worked myself into a position where I never wanted to be- removed from the people and neck deep in administrative paperwork. I was, to put it mildly, perpetuating systemic racism. That certainly is not the intention of the agency, or any other entities focused on improving the lives of those living in the conditions of poverty. But the services they provide are subject to the housing policies established before, during, and after the Civil Rights movement.

Today's income segregated neighborhoods were created by deliberate racially based policies, which is why I believe providing services (no matter how essential or well intentioned) reliant on this structure perpetuates systemic racism. The fact that those policies became illegal does not equate to these

24

neighborhoods gaining affluence. Which further exacerbates generational poverty among our country's 'lowest' income residents.

I hope these stories convey the helplessness felt among all the individuals floating, swimming, drowning, and keeping guard of the lives submerged in our societal trenches of poverty.

Chapter Two

Sitting Here in Limbo

As performed by Jerry Garcia and David Grisman

My longest employment engagement was at one of the many organizations striving to "end homelessness." Yup, a simple two-word statement encompassing unique values and a vision that attracts a beautiful breed of people committed to the task. The gratefulness for this job extended far beyond its paycheck. I was constantly humbled by our presence in the trenches of our society that is occupied by individuals most people have given up on.

There is a special appreciation for life when you share it with those living on, by, or off the actual streets. This agency serves anyone that no one else wants to. Not just in an economic class sense, but also in the field of homelessness, because it is primed as serving the 'hardest and most vulnerable to serve.' They provide public toilets for any individual to take a shit with some dignity- it would really be cold to have to shit outside during the chills of a Minnesota February (and probably embarrassing- oh, and a crime).

They also provide services to a wide spectrum of individuals and families living in the cyclical world of poverty. They see the scammers, the users, the mentally ill, the tired, the optimistic, the rising, and any another characteristic you can label an individual with. The commonality shared amongst all people is that we are human, and this makes us all flawed- with or without designations.

Sure, regular work issues and politics persist in such a place, but everyone has a sense that the world is bigger than themselves- and want to make sure life is better for everyone. The shared purpose is not to promote enabling or entitlement- but rather to empower people so that they can bask in the honor of being self-sufficient. That is not easy when having to adhere to federal, state, county, and city contract stipulations- all of which are determined by public and political perception. Sometimes these vital services end up providing entitlement or misappropriation- and even nothing at all.

I started work there in 2004- providing case management and rental assistance to families receiving state run public employment assistance- or 'welfare'- to all those fur coat wearing queens driving around in Escalades as they buy filet mignons.

In reality, most of this population is under educated and young. Countywide, I believe the statistic is in the ball park of 50-55% of the recipients do not have a high school diploma. It is also heavily represented by single mothers under the age 30... oh, and African American. There is the occasional single father, and sometimes a couple- and on rare occasions, actual 'married' couples. The population is also comprised of many non-English speaking, American Indian, Asian American, and white families.

The work history of most of these individuals is limited and sporadic- they are your order takers at your favorite fast food joint, the cleaning crews at the local sports arena, the fork lift drivers at the big box warehouses you frequent, the 'temps' that get called into your work for a 3 day stint, the cashiers at your grocery stores, the ticket takers at the movies, the janitors at any place that needs cleaning (especially toilets), security guards (or what do we call them? 'rent a cops') at the mall and downtown businesses, the 'weirdo' that took your money at the toll booth, the annoying person on your phone asking you to buy things- even though you thought you were on the do not call list- and a host of other $7.50 to $13 an hour paying jobs.

The agency's average for cases closing due to entering private market employment (or earning enough income to become ineligible to receive any more public assistance) is one of the highest in the county, and is around $11 an hour. About 15 to 20% of the caseload is able to reach that "self sufficient" benchmark each year.   All right, that gives you some background on the population, now it's story time.

One of my duties was to oversee 4 apartment units across the street from the office. The units were designated for families with 3 or more children coming out of a shelter with criminal background and/or chemical dependency issues that limited their ability to be housed in the private market (this population tended to also have multiple evictions and poor credit histories). So there I was, ready to help! Their housing was subsidized- they just needed my guidance to help them focus on treatment or employment goals so they could move right along and become self sufficient (I actually wasn't that naïve or self righteous, but I had never worked directly hands on before- and was both excited and nervous).

My heart ached for both the mother and children of one of the families I served. The mother had a heart of gold, but a history of falling back on a controlled substance habit every now and then. When this happened, she sometimes prostituted herself to be able to afford the habit (and it ain't a Pretty Women type of prostituting either- no Hollywood ending here). She had a charming personality and was so determined in wanting to do right- and expressed so much love for her children.

She really wanted a job and demonstrated this by showing up for job search, working on her resume, and applying for jobs- in this biz that is some real effort! She showed up and tried. Her criminal background was not warm and fuzzy. Not too many places are forgiving of anyone having a felony, let alone adding on a couple petty or regular misdemeanors related to economic and/or controlled substance crimes. This was kind of expected with the target population of the program. Tough to house, tough to employ. The fact that she was in her mid 30's and lacked of a high school diploma did not increase the likelihood of her obtaining private market employment anytime soon.

So after we made our formal introductions- it was time for me to help her develop a goal plan (I'm pretty sure this was not her first time at the "20 something white do gooder girl with a suburban up bringing trying to help fix her life because she just got her social worker license" rodeo before). This rodeo had a different spin. I was not a social worker, nor did I desire to become one- I found no use in being 'trained' to follow specific 'methods' and 'procedures' to 'help' people.

I was the youngest of my colleagues in the department. There were 6 of us, and my boss and I were the only 'whites.' All five of these people have made positive impacts in my life. My boss hired me on a whim, and told me something that still rings in my head today "you know, sometimes you may have a client and try to reach them and they don't respond- but it could be 10, 20 or 30 years later and they are able to draw on some of the advice you gave them."

The woman whose job I took over had transitioned into being a job counselor so that she could better utilize her Spanish speaking skills. This was my first encounter with someone so well educated and bursting with knowledge in this field. She was a force to reckon with, but her true desire to want to serve people, with doses of tough love empowerment, make her a true blessing. And then there was my boy 'On Demand'- he had a tendency to want you to stop whatever you were doing and come to his desk whenever summoned, but he, too, wants to help people improve their circumstance. And my word, he is also a prominent leader in the community outside of work- creating ways to deter young Somali men from acting out in unproductive ways.

And then there are the two ladies that demonstrated an insurmountable amount of respect for me in one of the worst situations I had to face. It is related to the lady mentioned above, who was one of my first 'cases' on the job. Things had been going 'great'—or at least for me. As I explained earlier, she was trying and trying AND trying! Eventually, a more seasoned co-worker was able to find a job for her from a renowned lady in the community that provides people with second, third—or really 'first' chances. But it was 8 or 9 months after of our introduction- she had been 'trying' without much luck for a long time- for not the first time in her life.

A day or two after the job connection, she was missing in action- relapsed back to a coping mechanism she knew could numb her despair. She was back on the streets. It had probably been a gradual transition, but without any telling signs for me to have noticed. I had developed a relationship with her children during home visits and helping with school stuff. They ranged from the ages 11 to 15; two boys and an 11-year-old girl. The boys were in afterschool programs and involved in sports- so it was just the girl that stopped at my desk around 3 o'clock one day.

She asked if I could let her into the apartment because her mom didn't come home the night before- and she didn't know where her brothers were. My heart sank- she said it as if it was just another day in the life, but I could see the fear and sadness in her eyes. We all knew where her mom was, and we also knew that we were in the position of being mandated reporters of child neglect- even though she came to see me (us) because she felt safe and familiar.

What happens when a child is abandoned? In this city, they are sent to Home for Children (code language for orphanage). How do they get there? Well, the law stipulates that service providers are not allowed to transport the children, instead the Home is notified and arranges police transportation- in their shear moment of abandonment, children are taken to a place with fellow children of abandonment, amongst unfamiliar adults to lord over them- until their parent, appointed guardian, or the child protection system takes over custodial duties.

At the time, I was not aware of this process. I didn't know what my role was, so I tried to cheer her up with compliments and engaging in light conversation (I was also processing what the Hell to do cuz I had no clue, and God bless my co-workers- my office mate observed the situation and informed the rest of the team). I casually opened her mother's file and started calling the listed emergency contact, but the line was disconnected. I then tried the park and school where her brothers might have been, but to no avail.

Then one my co-workers did her magic and invited the girl to go back to her office; to color, talk, and have a snack- you know loving and comforting stuff. My office mate walked over with a sympathetic look and told me to come over to my boss's office. Here I was (now allowed to show a bit of myself visibly shaken) in the company of my boss, my office mate, and another co-worker that seems to be a similar stone cold marshmallow like myself.

My boss delicately told me what the only option was. All three of them showed concern for my reaction and allowed a passable moment to pass for me to reflect before the marshmallow said- you know its almost 5 o'clock. Good Lord! Three of my four instant tag teamers were supposed to be long gone by now! The severity of the situation began sinking in. No one had an ounce of happiness in them, the room was somber- and nobody wanted to act on the situation.

We all agreed I should try all the phone numbers again. (I mean, its not like the 15 year old hadn't carried the load of this family before, perhaps we could pretend we never heard her say her mom hadn't been home the night before?). The two givers of insurmountable respect pulled me aside (Stone Cold Marshmallow and Ms. Magic) and told me that they would escort her to the police car for me.

They said they wanted to prevent me from the scorn of looking like some 20 something white do gooder escorting an African American child into the back of a squad car- for the whole neighborhood to see. I also think they did it for the girl. They wanted to use their courageous love and wisdom to comfort her as best as they could. After all, they were both African American and mothers; they were more culturally familiar to her and had more experience in providing such comfort.

I remember looking out the window and watching the moment. It was awful. No one talked about it and we all left. The next day we all hung our heads and made minimal eye contact. We were all processing it. I didn't even ask if the girl cried or not.

Chapter Three

Let Me Lie

As performed by Phish at Festival 8 (acoustic)

I hate to admit how in a weird way it was kind of cute to hear a little 4-year-old boy have a "fuck you" tantrum. Kids say the darndest things, right?

Most of my direct service experience has been working with low-income families, especially those with children and headed by women. Before I started working at the agency striving to "end homelessness"- I worked at a group home aimed at serving chemically dependent women in recovery, in the process of reunifying with their children whom they lost custody due to chemical dependency issues (wow, that's a mouth full).

Some described us as 'the eyes and ears' of child protection, but I never liked that description. I can describe this place of employment in one word "Yuck!" The close proximity to women at such a critical juncture in their life was too intense for me- so the yuck is not directed toward the place or the people it served, but the way it is systemically structured for the lives residing in it. It was also my first exposure to the negative impact that converging objectives of public assistance entities can have on people- when one would think they would be working in tandem for their benefit.

I will first give a description of the 3-story building. The second and third floors are filled with one-room suites (some connected), and large shared bathrooms for everyone's use. The attic is used as a storage facility for the belongings of clients who were either abruptly discharged or disappeared (staff get to haul it up there). The basement is space for food storage, laundry facilities, a childcare room, and a card shop (overseen by a gracious nun to provide the women a chance to earn a little cash by making greeting cards). The main floor houses most of the staff offices, a conference room, large kitchen connected to the dining room, living room, parlor, staff 'overnight' sleeping quarters, and the ever-popular 'PA' (or program assistant) office. The outside world has to buzz the PA office in order to be let in.

The place had an atmosphere designed for a '20 something white do gooder' approach. Or, the staffing positions were clearly designated as clinical or operational.   Hiring preference for clinical positions was given to licensed social workers and drug and alcohol counselors. While the more operational positions like the kitchen, childcare, and PA office; were usually staffed with program alumnae, hard knockers, and people without formal licenses. That is not to say there was a hard line in the sand between clinical and operational roles, because there was a lot of crossover and teamwork- but it created an interesting dynamic.

The part of line I have a hard time understanding is the benefit in having a young motherless person work one on one with mothers who obviously struggle with drug and/or alcohol issues to the point of losing custody of their children. The mere presence of them in this setting signifies the major juncture they face (can I get my child(ren) back?)- I wonder if the services rendered in such a setting may prove more effective with a different dynamic- that's all I'm saying.

It is in the one on one relationship with clinical staff where the client's articulate their long and short-term goals. Those meetings brought about an activity calendar for every client each week- that was used for the operational staff to monitor each person's comings and goings. They were required to sign in and out on the white board located in the PA office- and we would cross reference it with their approved passes (and take Urine Analysis samples when appropriate...while physically standing and watching them go to the bathroom).

There was little to no room for relapse in this setting. The building was staffed 24 hours 7 days a week. The nights and weekends were equipped with one PA to man the entire house- and a phone number to the rotating 'beeper,' which connected us to clinical staff whenever situations warranted advisement. Depending on which staff had the beeper, you would get a call back right away or within an hour or two. I seldom used the beeper during situations, but felt obligated to use it once a situation was diffused (I guess to formally report on it).

Operational staff was suggested to use the beeper whenever a client acted out. Here is a phone call example of a warranted situation "...um, so and so was assigned to set up dinner tonight- she is not here and her activity pass says she should be back by now- what should I do?"... "Find someone else to set up dinner." There were many of times I either set up the pre made meal, or was able to find another resident to do it. The beat went on and tummies were fed- and clinical staff would deal with the client behavior during business hours.

Some other warranted situations involved clients getting into skirmishes against one other or relying on the PA office to 'watch' their kid(s) longer than the agreed 15 or 20 minute relief period. Things really heated up and jumped off the chain when the house was put on mandatory restriction- meaning no one was allowed to leave the house for any reason aside from court mandated activities.

Whew, the PA staff did not look forward to weekend shifts during a mandatory restriction. I think management called them retreats- we called them lockdown...

Imagine the frustration felt in being constantly cooped up with the same people in the same 'tight' space while going through such an emotional and stressful time in your life. And not having any real control over it. Ugh- you spill your beans together in daily 'group' therapy sessions, accommodate daily routines to share bathroom spaces, rotate and oversee each others daily house chore duties (and tell on people that do a sloppy or inadequate job), and share a bond in figuring out what inner strength you have to get your children back into your custody- so that you to are able to live on your own again. It is easy to see how overwhelming one could feel in such a setting.

This population also had some history together outside of the group home- there's always a little drama behind everything. In fact, I didn't know at the time when these two particular ladies briefly resided together (one was completing the program and the other had just arrived). The one nearing program completion was the 'cheated' in a love triangle involving her, the new arrival, and the same male. It was not uncommon for different tensions to swell up amongst residents, but even with hindsight- I can say both of these ladies left their wounds of betrayal outside of the building. Coincidently, the new arrival also became the 'cheated' with the same guy in a different love triangle.

The "Fuck You" tantrum by the 4-year-old boy occurred during one of those weekend retreats. His mother had a lifelong battle with alcohol, and was embarking on her 5th or 6th bout of maintaining sobriety. She was a quiet one and never ruffled any feathers.

Her mother and brother were strong pillars of support- they provided her with transportation and dropped off essential household needs or snacks (especially during lockdown). Although these favors, and their actual physical presence, wasn't as frequent as some systems of support for other residents- because they lived outside of the city.

During this weekend mandatory restriction, the brother was coming to pick up the boy so he could at least take a break from the tenacious surroundings. He didn't want to leave his mom, and cut a rug kicking and screaming while yelling many, "Fuck You(s)." The innocence of his little voice took the vulgarity out of the phrase, but the apparent infliction of pain in his tantrum made my heart sink. It was obvious he had been through a lot in his 4 years on this earth. His mother was near her own breaking point, but remained calm as she repeatedly told him that it was only for a little while, and that he would have fun playing games with his uncle and grandmother.

Once the boy left, she shut the door to the PA office before taking a seat. I said nothing. Frustration, guilt, and fear were written all over her face- and shining through her sad eyes. She then admitted, "I don't even know what to do." I told her she was doing fine, and then let her talk through the confusion and fear that brought her to this moment. She explained how the demands of her child protection worker, job counselor, and the group home made her feel like she was always failing. She remarked how bad she felt for everything she had put her son through (we shared a smile when said she had no idea where he picked up the phrase "Fuck You"). She also said she was scared of the idea of making it on her own because of her lack of employment experience and education.

42

Her sincerity moved me- and I told her that. I also reminded her how calm she remained during her son's tantrum and that she was one of the very few residents that never got 'written up'- and always completed her job duties to the fullest. We both reaffirmed the truth that this was only a temporary moment in her life. She thanked me for my time and went back into her routine.

She tracked me down a couple years later and asked me to write a letter of recommendation for her to get into permanent section 8 housing. I was thrilled, not just because of her new opportunity; but also because she thought highly enough of me to ask for a recommendation. I quickly agreed and sent the letter off. I received a call from the landlord shortly after, and got to speak favorably on her behalf directly to the deliberating party. She got in, and was very happy for the direction her life was taking. Another 'dirty' secret about us in human services is that we care about the lives we touch- no matter how ugly or beautiful the circumstance is when we're involved.

A couple years ago, I had lunch with two dear friends I worked with at the group home (we all hightailed it out of there around the same time). After catching up on each other's personal lives, we inquired and informed one other on the whereabouts of some past clients. I'm not sure if it was at this lunch or one of my few 'drop-ins' at the actual group home- but it was around this time that I learned the women, with the 4-year-old F bomb dropping son, had fallen off the wagon and lost custody her son (this time, probably for 'good'- or permanently).

That was not the first (or last) time I was either made aware or saw a mother loose custody of her child(ren). The 'new arrival' mentioned earlier had a hard time following the routine. She would be out longer than approved on her pass, have guests visit during non-visiting hours (and not obey the PAs when told to ask the guests to leave), get into personality clashes with other residents (and staff), and complete some of her daily chores inadequately.

I believe the 'swab' U.A. test came back positive when she arrived from one of her weekend passes. We still had to wait for the actual sample to be sent to the lab to get a more thorough chemical analysis breakdown. We had a Monday morning meeting of both clinical and operational staff to discuss our next move. Her child protection worker was made aware of the situation, and was waiting to here if the client would be allowed to reside in the group home or not.

The ultimate decision fell on the program manager, but our interactions and observations on how this client was doing had to be taken into consideration (perhaps as a means to gather 'justifiable' evidence?) The snarkiness of the comment in parenthesizes is directed more toward the actual program manager at the time, rather than the process itself. I can't even count how many times she used the metaphor "give 'em enough rope and they'll hang themselves" whenever we expressed concern of individual client progressions. I personally think that such an approach and sentiment is counterproductive to providing people with a second chance in life.

Anyway, we're sitting in this processing meeting- and everyone is in agreement that this client is not working the program very well, and is becoming a bad influence on the other residents. The decision was made that she should be discharged. The way in which she would be discharged was not discussed, and might have been one of the most counterproductive means to actual healing I've seen in my life.

The PA office had a big window that peered into the living room where the client and her children were sitting on a couch. I think only the case manager was made aware of what was about to occur, and the rest of us were totally left in the dark when two fully uniformed county sheriff officers were buzzed in.

The case manager opened the living room door, looked down at the ground, and quietly summoned the client to come out of the living room- as the two officers stood behind her.

All the residents in the living room had knee jerk reactions of alertness (yet calm) and wrapped their arms around their children (and tucked their young faces into their chests). All of us witnessing this in the PA office were shocked and scared- is this is what we agreed to? The client began crying and asking why? Why? The program manager stepped in and used a more forceful voice in telling the client to come over.

The client was a wreck, but began ushering her kids toward the door. The program manager interrupted this movement "No, leave the kids- just you, come take a step out here" The client was now very confused and squeezed her kids and told them she loved them. The program manager grabbed the client's hand and pulled her over to the other side of the hall while the two officers went into the living room and picked up each of the kids.

The kids were now in tears, the other residents and their kids were in tears, and the rest of us staff could not believe what we were seeing! We watched the parade of kids with flailing arms reaching out toward their mother, while being carried out of the house by the officers- as their mother collapsed to the ground in tears.

Nobody said a word for a few minutes. Once the children were gone, the client was told to pack up her belongings. I don't think child protection was happy with how it shook out. Hell, I don't think the officers or anyone else involved liked it. I know for certain that the case manager was very upset, but at least the client was discharged and sent back out on the streets, right? Too bad both she and her children had to go through such a dramatic ordeal. Seriously, if I only knew then what I know now…

It wasn't always that bad. I guess you could say there were even "better off for the kid" separations that happened in more constructive ways. One that stands out is the tale of 'Baby Badass.' Man, he would barrel his 2-year-old body into a room like a running back giving a one-two touchdown punch. He would demand toys from other kids, head butt adults, and leave bite marks on many human bodies.

But underneath all of that aggression was a little baby boy with striking blonde hair and fiery blue eyes. He became just as happy and curious with shiny objects, playful coos, and animated facial expressions as any other 2-year-old. I will admit that he was definitely a handful, but this little firecracker stole a place in my heart. He was very smart, and constantly pointed at objects or people while trying to form words. His mother was very young and mad at the world. She was in her early 20's with a mouth full of dentures- as a result of frequent meth use. She became easily agitated and ready to go toe to toe with anyone she felt threatened by.

She was slowly working the program, and trying to not yell at her son all the time. She knew it wasn't a good idea to call him a 'piece of shit' or an 'idiot'- and was now at least taking a deep breath when she got frustrated, instead of belting out mean spirited assaults toward him. There was one incident where I thought his shoulder was going to come out of socket when she hastily picked him up by his right forearm. Anyway, she had gotten to the point of no longer insulting or physically treating him that way in front of staff, but I cannot guarantee what happened behind closed doors. His cries were never sobs- they were howls.

During my tenure, I switched from being a childcare worker to a PA. Which resulted in my 100% transition to PA having a little more 'kid watching' time than most PA's. I didn't mind it as long as I didn't have to prep a meal or haul someone's belongings up to storage (in addition to the other PA duties). One day, long after the "let them hang themselves" program manager, I was working a daytime PA shift. You were called on to do a lot more during those shifts, and I usually kept my kid watching arrangements to a minimum.

It was Baby Badass's birthday, and his mom jubilantly stopped by the PA office first thing in the morning. She was talking about his celebration plans later that day, and he was dressed to the nines! It was without hesitation that I agreed to watch (or cuddle) with him while she made a quick trip to the corner store. It would only be 15 minutes, and I didn't have anything pressing to do at the moment. Well, 15 minutes soon turned into an hour, then two, then four...and then it was 3 o'clock. I couldn't believe it, what could have happened?

It was spring or summer, because I remember sitting with him on the front steps to get some fresh air. He was in my lap and my arms were around him as we listened to birds and watched the world go by. I remember thinking- where is your mom? How could she do this to you? Really, on your birthday? This isn't real is it? Who could ever abandon you?

When I went inside, I learned the arrangements his child protection worker made, and that his grandmother would be picking him up shortly. I had met his grandmother a few times, and knew she was genuinely concerned for both her daughter and grandson- and really wanted her daughter to get better. But always demonstrated her front and center concern for the well being of her grandson. After all, she was the one who originally called child protection on her daughter because of the life she was exposing him to. This was probably the best arrangement for everyone (I hope).

There were no dramatic tears or staff in shock when this custody swap happened. It was almost a sense of relief. We never heard from his mother, and she never returned to pick up her belongings. I suppose that gave me something to do, because I was one of the staff that packed and moved all her belongings to the storage unit in the attic (she had lots of pictures of him and his framed artwork). I hope Baby Badass is having fun being a happy and curious kid- maybe someday he'll be in the NFL.

Chapter Four

Fast Train

As performed by Solomon Burke

Sometimes when you don't act on, or even contemplate, a doubt- it can manifest into a belief that it's just how things go. It was not until my 6th year of employment at the agency trying to "end homelessness" that I did a 'shelter' tour. This tour humbled me into a world I was close to, yet unfamiliar with.

There was a shelter located in the basement where I worked- literally below my desk. I had strolled through the digs and walked past many of the guests numerous times, but only during non-operational hours. That is, the shelter opens each night at 5 pm and closes every morning at 7 am. I had gone in and out of work during those hours or on weekends, but rarely ventured downstairs to see it in action.

One day, as I leaving the office on a Sunday afternoon, I exchanged the usual pleasantries with a guest who added "There goes the hardest working girl in the agency"- a bit of an exaggeration, but we shared a laugh and smile together. He had observed me coming in and going multiple times, and each time I had observed him waiting and reading- in the parking lot. I guess you could say that he is one of the many 'hardest' workingmen on the streets.

I should mention that tons of my former colleagues are well educated and bursting with knowledge. Their education and knowledge varies in type and vehicles to express it. The school of hard knocks is just as insatiable in merit and worth as the school of celebrated formal education (or Universities). Similarly, it is just as powerful to share knowledge in an overt manner, as it is noble to share it through silent expressions of action. And the mixed bag combination of education and knowledge types, in conjunction with different vehicles to express it, make it a pretty balanced operation.

One of these mixed bag combinations leads (amongst many other endeavors) shelter tours for anyone interested. These tours consist of stops at some of the most vital pit stops in the city for people living on the streets (or in the condition of poverty). The tour

52

begins at the Monday night lottery for the three private single adult shelters, then stops at the two large family shelters, goes to a youth daytime drop-in center, and ends at the bottom rung hub for single adults not lucky enough to win at the lottery- but at least they don't have to sleep in the streets- which is considered rock bottom (or illegal).

It should also be noted that such a tour must be taken with caution. It has a "visitor staring at animals in the zoo" type of dynamic. Imagine strangers peering into your world while trying to locate a place to shelter your head during the private hours of night. But taking one provides a full sense of the unbelievable conditions our society allows to persist in these trenches.

The shelter lottery is much more desolate than the bright lights and dings-dings found at a casino. On this night, I believe there was something like 15 slots available for over 100 adults attempting to seek refuge. Most of the faces in the room were familiar to each other, except for us tourists. The coveted prize sought was a 28-day reservation for a bed at one of the 3 privately run single adult shelters in the city- located in church basements.

These are the Ritz Carlton's of shelters for single adults- compared to the other options. Whenever I went into the basement at work (which is one of the Ritz's) I was reminded of summer camp. It is one large room lined with wood paneled walls and filled with several metal bunk beds containing one-inch thick green rubber mats. The egress windows provide glimmers of sunshine onto the worn linoleum tiled checkered floor... There is a kitchen and pantry where guests are assigned to the various meal duties. There is also a 'rec' room with a pop machine, some couches, and a T.V. When temperatures are extremely frigid, they open up the shelter early, but cannot do this with regularity since volunteers make up a significant amount of the shelter staff.

The lottery is located in one of the church basements. The set up looks like a bingo hall. There is a section of a few tables in front for staff that run perpendicular to several more tables and chairs for potential winners. The place was packed, and very few potential winners took their coat off to get comfortable. There was a stale chatter of restlessness before staff announced the festivities would begin. The same wire rimmed circular case containing bingo balls is used to pick the evening 'winners.'

The advantage of being called early allows for shelter preference. At one point a man got up and started yelling at the staff because he thought they had rigged the system. The staff politely explained the policy of it's on call list. Another staff in the crowd pulled him aside to further explain so that the lottery could continue. The actual slot drawing takes about 10 or 15 minutes.

There is some joy expressed by the winners, but it is more of a temporary relief than pure elation. The rest of the disenfranchised gamblers slowly disperse up the stairs and back out into the streets. Our tour stopped at the 'donation' closet before leaving the basement.

Just like at the Ritz Carlton, this storage closet is filled with boxes of travel-sized toiletries. The box containing brand new underwear is near empty compared to the many boxes filled with shampoo. I know I am privileged enough to put on a clean pair of underwear everyday, and had not realized how dignified that is until I stood in that closet. The boxes designated for new socks and t-shirts are just as empty.

As we headed out the doors, I noticed a man who was in a subsidized work program- doing janitorial duties around the office I worked. His face was not as happy (nor mine) as at our daily exchanges. Every morning when I arrived at work I was greeted with a "GGGGGooood Mornin! - How's Ms. Katie doing?...I'm doing alright, I'm alive; and you?...I'm doing great- the sun is shining!" We would tell each other to not work too hard while sharing a smile and quick laugh together.

Our pleasant "how's it going?" banter did not seem appropriate. And there certainly was no reason for us to ask each other either why we were there. Instead we made earnest, yet hollow eye contact with toothless smiles, as we quietly said "hi."

Next stop- the family shelters! The difference between single adult and family shelters is like that of night and day. There are a lot more resources being directed toward family shelters. We physically went to the county funded one and did a drive by of the privately funded one. Lucky (or not so lucky) for me, I've been to both multiple times; and will draw on distinctions between their similarities and differences.

The two largest family shelters in the city are similar stand alone structures (not church basements). They are buildings reminiscent of a hotel, yet each room is either a studio or one bedroom with all the amenities of an apartment. The private shelter quantitatively has larger units (2 or 3 bedrooms) than the county funded one. Both of their 'greeting' centers are anything but grand hotel entrances. Instead, they echo the type of entryway found in correctional facilities. You go through metal detectors, check in with security (and if you don't have a badge or something legitimizing your visit, you wait for the guest to meet you) and then pass through a subway turnstile. The space in each of these facilities is also floored with linoleum.

In order to get into the county shelter, the head of household goes down to epicenter for public assistance to get 'vouchered' in. To be vouchered in, means your monthly public assistance cash grant and food stamps are transferred to the shelter. If a family is working and not receiving employment assistance, they are charged a daily (out of pocket) rate of $30 a night. Approval is based on meeting the eligibility requirements of facing (or at imminent risk of facing) homelessness, having custody of children, and meeting a very low percentage of the area median income- oh and most importantly, if there is room in the shelter.

There is also an actual hotel that the county utilizes for overflow- or, it is really a motel that is called a hotel. Each family that enters the county funded shelter system receives services. That is, they are assigned case managers to expedite their transition from staying in the shelter into housing. I believe a recent average stay for a family in the county shelter is around 3 to 4 months, which is not the same at the private shelter.

The county does not have a formal relationship with the owner of the private shelter; and she is allowed to set her own terms and conditions on who gets to come in, how long they stay, and how much they will have to pay. One of the major downsides of this arrangement is that residents are not assigned a county funded worker, so the stays tend to be much longer without the extra resources and access to subsidies- more around the 6 to 12 month range. On the other hand, it is 'easier' to get in and payment arrangements can be made that best suit the family and their situation.

I worked with families from both shelters, and it does not matter which one they stay at- the actual exiting out of a shelter into private market housing does have not the same glitz and glamour some people feel when moving into a new place.

In fact, one time I received a call from a landlord- she informed me that a client of ours (who was scheduled to move into one of her units that day) was sitting beside a snow bank with all of her belongings, because the apartment was unwilling to sign the subsidy paperwork. Again, it was that 3 o'clock hour...and her caseworker was out and no one else seemed to have a minute to spare- so off I went.

I couldn't shake the image of someone sitting on a curb next to all of his or her possessions- without a place to go or any transportation- in the middle of winter. Hell, the county had paid for the cab that dropped her off there- but the cab rides are only one way (talk about expediting a fast exit!). I knew there was no way for the cabby or the county know what was going on, so I located the client's phone number and called her on my way out there. I didn't have a plan, but I wasn't going to leave her stranded in a cold moment of abandonment.

I asked her why she was sitting out in the cold, and she responded, "what am I supposed to do, this is everything I own" (Duh- I'd been out of direct service a bit too long to consider the obvious before opening my mouth). A few hours earlier, she had packed up all her belongings and stuffed them into a cab for the half hour drive to her new digs. After unloading everything (she had just loaded), she found out she couldn't move in. I asked how long she'd been sitting on the curb and she said for almost two hours.

We barley fit everything in the trunk, back seat, and floor of the front seat in my Jetta. She was a bit distraught. Originally transportation was arranged for her kids to be dropped off at the apartment, and she had just finished rearranging it so they would be dropped off at the shelter- but she was not vouchered in at this point, and did not know what she would do after meeting up with her kids. I figured we had a car ride and my cell phone to sort out those logistics. But first I'd try talking to the landlord, and see if this rejection was a misunderstanding.

Basically a communication breakdown had occurred between the case manager and apartment management. The landlord asserted that they (located in a suburb outside of the agency's established landlord network) didn't realize they had to sign a contract agreement with the agency in order to receive the subsidy. I asked if they accepted subsidies, and she said "yes- just not binding ones." I asked if an inspection was performed on the unit and she answered "yes- but I didn't realize that meant we had to sign off on anything..."

Simplistically speaking, there are two types of rental assistance subsidies available: short term 'shallow' subsidies that don't require signatures, and long term 'deep' subsidies that do. Shallow and deep refer the dollar amount. The long and deep subsidies require a lot more paperwork, and each unit must pass a Housing Quality Standards inspection. I was trying to draw on that distinction to see if she'd fold, but to her it was moot point- so we quietly left.

As we settled into the car, I realized how calm she was in spite of her situation. Up to this point she had spoken very little. I could see the determined angst in her eyes. You know, the kind where you just want to surrender yourself to a kicking and screaming tantrum filled with tears and swear words, but instead remain stoic and try to remember it's just a temporary time in life.

I was not going to dismiss her aggravation with attempts to cheer her up with funny one-liners or frivolous small talk (in some ways I represented one of the entities that got her into this situation). So I apologized, explained how we were new to the neighborhood (so to speak); and that regardless of who's at fault- it can only be described as a shitty situation. Oh, and that she was doing an amazing job keeping herself together.

This opened her up to at talking about how upset and disappointed she was- how she didn't have family or friends to stay with, how she thought she would be moved in and making dinner by now, how she didn't know if she would be able to stay at the shelter that night, and how she didn't have a car or any money to get her and her kids somewhere even if she had place to go.

We were interrupted by a call from my co-worker informing me that she was vouchered in for the night. Again, not much elation; but a sense of temporary relief filled the air. We pulled up to the shelter. She headed toward the entrance to sign some paperwork and grab a cart to move all her belongings back into the building. I began unloading her things and setting them by the curb.

It was a busy hour in front on the shelter (people coming back from work or waiting for their kids to come home on afterschool buses). Her trip took longer because folks were 'shocked.' "Girl...I thought you were moving out today!?!...Are you kidding me?!...Oh I'm sorry baby!" I felt like a misplaced deal breaker in their world of empathy and confusion- I understood perfectly well what had happened. They were trying to sort through it without having all the contractual and subsidy information I possess. But I certainly was not going to show off my 'chops.' I let them sort through it with the information they had. Hell, it was more her experience than mine- so what could I add?

Pretty soon there were 3 or 4 other people unloading the Jetta. We were silent and focused on the task. Men, women, and children brought her belongings through the turnstile and back into her temporary residence of the night. We exchanged goodbyes, and I drove to the same house I had lived in for almost 7 years.

Next stop on the shelter tour was the youth drop-in center. This was, without a doubt, the most aesthetically pleasing dwelling we visited that night. It was in the middle of a reconstruction project- with a high ceilinged circular floor to ceiling stone fireplace. It was spectacular, and a far cry away from memories of summer camp or hotels with turnstile entrances.

This was the only facility we stopped at that was not a residence; but rather, a drop-in center. Teens can stop by anytime from 8 in the morning to 8:30 at night. There is a computer lab, some classrooms, an industrial kitchen connected to a dinning room, and a 'rec' room. Staff is onsite to provide services ranging from basic healthcare to locating housing. It was a ghost town when we arrived around the 8 o'clock hour.

Throughout the tour, our guide encouraged us to ask any questions (no matter how ridiculous) and patiently answered each and every one of them. She has, after all, been in the biz long enough to witness the evolution of Prince changing his name from 'Prince' to the 'Artist Formerly Known as Prince' and back to 'Prince.' So she knows a thing or two about homelessness, especially in this city and the state as a whole. She had completed 3 years of medical school, and was preparing for her residency when she decided to change careers. I asked what caused the switch- she said walking into one of the church basement shelters.

We were now headed to our final destination for the evening, the bottom-rung juggernaut of lodgings for single adults that don't win at the lottery. I mentioned being humbled by this tour (and that is true in its whole sense), but I must say that this stop horrified me. I cannot believe this is 'how it goes.' I will try to describe it as best as I can, and I may have some of the technical stuff confused- but the inhumane conditions I bore witness far outweigh any impact of 'factual' semantics.

Basically, there is a two building community that has various 'last resort' shelter options. One of the buildings is a first come first serve- and pay to stay- operation. Remember the summer camp aura of the church basement shelter? Well a memory of that is all you can carry in here. It is a much larger space, but the density of metal bunk beds containing one-inch thick green rubber mats is quite staggering in comparison. The church basement shelters have about 4 to 5 feet in between each bunk; this space has about 4 to 5 inches. Every bunk is utilized every night.

We stopped on a men's floor- and every single age, race, and other characteristic was represented. Everyone was grabbing the solace of privacy in their bed, their space for the night (with their life possessions able to fit in a rented locker the size of a small gym locker)- if they were lucky enough to get one.

As we walked to the next building, on the connecting sidewalk, I walked with flashbacks of the yearning eyes watching us watch them. There was a police presence as well as lines of adults waiting to get into the building we were headed. I saw the supported work guy waiting in the line, and he saw me. This time we both just nodded and looked at the ground. I wasn't giving him a look of sympathy, nor was he giving me a look of helplessness – rather, we exchanged eyes of empathetic dissatisfaction. We never spoke of that night to each other, what is there to say?

The first stop, in the last building of the night, was a women's floor that also had a 'medical' section. The rooms are the same size as those of a hospital, and the mattresses are much thicker than their green rubber counterparts- but the amount of beds stuffed into each room is way more than that of a standard hospital. The medical staff that attends to the disabled women is sparse and mostly work daytime hours. And if you are a non-disabled, you are either lucky enough to get a one-inch thick green rubber mat or a possible hospital equivalent mattress- to sleep under the fluorescent lights in the hallways.

Out of all the stops this evening, this was the most bustling. Several women approached us and wanted to show us how and where they lived. They didn't expect us to do anything- they just wanted to tell their story, and we listened. At least they were off the streets that night, right?

The final stop of the night still haunts me. I forget the exact floor it is located, but that is how it is known around town (or on the streets). This was the only stop where the occupants weren't settling into their space for the evening, because it was the last resort and they were still in a line outside waiting to get in (if they were lucky).

There was the usual linoleum, but no metal bunk beds- just one-inch thick green rubber mats placed directly on the floor without any inches or feet to separate them. Packed in like sardines in not an understatement. Rows and rows of a green sea filled the room. I imagined being stuck in the middle or on the far end of the sea- and having to get up to go to the bathroom- crawling over people and disturbing their sleep. I also imagined how ridiculous it is that being placed in such a situation might seem luxurious as opposed to being out on the cold streets.

And then I thought about any possessions I'd want to keep on my body- such as an Ipod (music has been known to soothe me), and how sleeping in such close proximity with so many other people may deter me from wanting something so valuable- not out of fear of theft, but out of lack of physical 'privacy.' I'm glad no one was in there, because I would not have been able to handle adding a human element to that spectacle- the imagination was enough.

(Un) fortunately, they let the old and disabled in before everyone else, so we got to see a couple gentlemen with canes settle into their space. Their mattresses were placed outside of the sea. They were both up there in age and obviously harboring great physical discomfort. Watching them situate themselves (without assistance) onto one of those green mats is nothing I ever want to see again.

How can this be? This happens every night! These are the lucky ones since their mats are placed on the perimeter of the sea of green? No pillow? No blankets? Just a sheet (maybe). I couldn't help but make brief eye contact with one of the gentlemen; there was no bitterness or pain in his eyes- just despondence.

We left the building as all the other guests were entering. We had a solemn car ride back to the office. When I got out of the van, the guy I always see waiting and reading in the parking lot was outside. We both said hello- paused a moment to take in the night, and then said "see ya tomorrow." I got in my car and drove back to my house-with a European pillow top king sized mattress donned in 300 plus thread count bedding, and 1200 square feet to place any of my belongings (wherever I want)- and laid my head down in the privacy of my own world (with my dog).

Chapter Five

Mohammed's Radio
As performed by Warren Zevon

One day, a case manager of one of the single adult programs stopped by my office. I was talking to another staff about subsidy stuff- he apologized for interrupting, but wanted to let me know that one of his clients had died- and would no longer need a check sent out on his behalf. I froze and was momentarily paralyzed as a chill ran through my body.

He was not looking directly at me, rather sort of behind me with his chin up (very stoic). I muttered a concerned "what?" And he repeated the same thing. I still didn't think I heard him right, "are you kidding me? How?" He said he didn't know, but the police think he had been dead in his apartment hallway for over two weeks. He then looked me in the eyes and said "just wanted to let you know so you don't send out a check next month" (I think it was the 2nd or 3rd of the month- concerns over next months checks were no where on the horizon). I told him I was so sorry to hear that- I didn't know what to say, but I could definitely feel his sorrow...

He left the office, I wanted to follow him; but I didn't... and continued fumbling through subsidy stuff- with silent grief underlying our exchange. Two other people worked in the same office with me. One of them used to be a case manager in a program similar to bearer of sad news guy. When this office mate arrived, I told him what happened (and the client name).

He froze (he had worked with the client). He then regained himself and asked questions of the how and why. Was he found in his apartment hallway or the hallway in his apartment building? How could nobody of found him for two weeks? Who found him? I didn't know the answer to any of these questions, and the same ones had been festering in my head. Prior to this, I only knew the client by name because I issued his rent check each month. And then my office mate shared more sorrowful information.

The client had been cut off from his family (or the more caring relatives were deceased or out of contact) so there was probably no one to call...no one to tell that would care. And even more distressing of a thought- no one to make sure he would receive a proper burial.

We then spoke of concern for the case manager. When did he last see him? My office mate shared that the client did really well when his ducks were in a row, but sometimes floundered- and wondered what type of 'state' the client was in when this happened. Throughout the week, other staff would trickle in and mention the incident, and we would be at a loss of words before mentioning our condolences to both the client and the case manager.

Nobody knew what was going on. Was any family found? Did anyone know more about how it happened? What's going to happen? Are we going to have to put on a service? How is the case manager taking it? Has he said anything to you? The case manager's office was at another site so we did not see him everyday.

When I finally heard him passing through the hall I told my office mate to go talk to him (they at least shared the experience of both working with this particular population and the actual client). I'm not sure what was exchanged, but they spoke for a bit and my office mate said he was fine. I believed him and left it at that.

This is not the first time a person has died without familial ties to ensure a proper burial. Here is an excerpt from an internal staff email:

> *Anyone know of resources to help someone in poverty pay for her mom's funeral? She is not currently homeless, and not working directly with us.*

This email received plenty of responses, and created a 'loose' protocol for such instances.

> *For anyone who faces this question in the future, each county has a program to help cover funeral costs. Most funeral homes also have the funds available. Certain agencies may also make funds available on a case-by-case basis. Local religious congregations often have benevolence funds to help with family crises, although these are often limited to members of the congregation. If the person who died was in "program" housing, that agency may have funds to help. For Native American folks, Indian Ministries used to help but their funds have been cut so maybe less likely, but worth a shot; also try the person's reservation.*

Lastly, if the person is a program participant here, we have a limited amount of "emergency money" for things like this. See the Keeper of the Dough.

The average life expectancy for someone homeless is less than that of someone not homeless. Years of living on the street (submerged deep in the conditions of poverty) may cause someone to struggle with untreated chronic health problems, like diabetes or mental illness, because of the lack of access to proper treatment and traditional healthcare remedies.

Every year organizers put on a memorial march to honor the homeless persons that died during that year. In 2010, the organizers counted over 100 individuals that died while struggling with issues of homelessness in this state- a number higher than the year before. One of the organizers (who plays a integral role in gathering the names of the fallen) was quoted as saying "We do it to bring dignity to people who sought it during their lives"... "We do it to hold them close once again."

A formerly homeless person was also quoted as saying, "the worst thing about being homeless was the feeling that no one cared"

Another gem of wise knowledge stopped by my office to talk about a collaborative effort, with a few other agencies, to provide employment services to the homeless single adults living in the city. It had not been a smooth transition, and she stopped by to update me on the phone and Internet situation at her new offsite location.

I might as well shed a little light on how this agency's approach to servicing clients is unique to other providers in the field. This lady was hired to run an employment program for anyone staying in the three private single adult shelters- the program evolved and eventually began servicing anyone who walked in the door.

When you agree to 'meet people where they are at' you take on the risk of not having stellar outcomes. Almost any funder wants tangible proof that their money went toward something that made a positive impact. Most funding tied to employment, or job training, requires a certain percentage of a caseload obtaining employment as a result of the program (usually around 80% of a caseload) to be considered a 'success.'

Such a benchmark may steer the focus away from helping anyone, to helping those that will boost your outcomes- so this particular program relies on in-kind donations rather than contractual funding, to make sure they can 'meet people where they are at'- because for some people, participating in this type of environment provides them with a sense of dignity.

One guy literally stuffed hundreds of plastic bags up each of his sleeves 'just in case' someone needed one. He would come to the job room everyday and search the web for an hour and a half, because that was what he did Monday through Friday. The likelihood of him being hired anywhere seemed unlikely, but he treated his daily Internet surfing like a job. He showed up on time, followed all the computer and job room rules- and left at his scheduled 'quit' time.

In a sense, it provided him with an obligation of something to do everyday- a reason to get out of bed and take a shower. At home, he habitually got parking tickets for parking his car by a meter outside of his apartment (and diligently fought to appeal each one). He was also a pack rat, and his habitually ticketed car was filled to the gills with 'things.' I don't think he drove to many places other than his apartment and the job room. He was also always getting in trouble for feeding bread to pigeons. A nearby company was so furious and complained that they had to replace an AC unit because of all the bird shit. Not sure where he is today, because the landlord had it with the parking ticket and bird poop drama. Hopefully, he's somewhere where he is able to at least maintain his daily hour and a half Internet routine.

74

In addition to welcoming 'job' program environments, a housing first model (house people and then provide follow up supportive services to address needs) is both vital and effective to 'meet people where they are at.' This agency's housing first programs rely on private market landlords, and could perhaps be more effective with more lenient landlords. They do the best they can, and have an impressive landlord network; but it is not perfect. One of the housing first programs, targeting the most vulnerable and hardest to serve in the city, has participants averaging a 'decade' amount of time living in the streets.

They are no strangers to the county jail, detox and emergency rooms. And the agency works closely with local law enforcement, as well as the county court and hospital systems, to help identify people for referral. This effort gets people off the street and into housing- and then assists them in accessing whatever public assistance they are eligible to get the proper medical and therapeutic services to become stabilized- this approach is proven to drive down public costs with drastically fewer jail, detox and emergency room visits.

Sometimes word travels on the street that a fellow 'street' buddy got an apartment, and other struggling individuals take advantage of the situation- and camp out in the cozy space...

The lady that stopped by my office also talked about how the 'regulars' were reacting to the new job room collaborative. This led us to talking about former clients, and since remembering people can remind you of other people- memories started flooding the conversation. Which led to this horrible story.

A guy that stayed in the shelter five years earlier went through her job program. He was eventually housed with a subsidy and moved into an apartment. In recent times, she received a call from another alumni who said "you've got to go check on so and so- I stopped by there and he is basically dying- with a bunch of crack heads and drunks taking over his living room." She contacted his case manager, who had been over there 5 or 6 times in the past couple months; but no one answered the phone or door- and she couldn't get a hold of the landlord. The urgency of the alumni's call prompted her to feverishly knock on the door until it opened (her next move was to call the police)...

The two people that opened the door said the client was sick in his bed. She described him as looking as though he hadn't showered in at least two months, and was so weak that he couldn't even lift his head. She immediately called an ambulance. Doctors estimated that he had been internally bleeding for months, and that (undiagnosed) cancer had taken over his body to the point of no return. He had periodically been given food by his visiting squatters, but had evidently puked up every bite of it. He weighed about 80 pounds, half of his normal weight. He was moved to hospice, and lived the rest of his life in and out of coherence.

There was no readily available information to call family or kin- he didn't know their current contact information. He requested a specific shelter advocate to come sing for him (and she did). The request for the landlord to change the locks, to prevent further squatting, was countered with a $200 fee. People finally tracked down his brother- who hadn't seen him in 6 years, and he gathered family members to be with him for the last few days of his life.

The lady in charge of the job room program said she could not bring herself to go see him at the hospital, partly because she didn't want to exacerbate his mental condition- almost all of the clients she serves call her "Ma." It should also be noted that anyone who enters her program is under no obligation to continue- there is no housing or any other incentive attached to it- they do it because they want to.

And what about the two people that finally answered the door? He called them friends. Friends that didn't call an ambulance, friends that didn't answer the door, friends that let people enter his apartment for booze and drug binges, friends that stopped by his hospital bed to ask for money. Yes, they were friends to him because they showed up and acknowledged him. They were there for him. The case manager did not question his view in calling them 'friends'- because that is what he believed, and if that is what he held onto- let him.

Up until his brother was tracked down, the majority of people he was around (that truly cared about him) were paid to do so. And maybe the squatters are genuinely good people since they tried to feed him soup. Perhaps they are caught up in the vicious cycle and tragic reality of drug addiction. He never personally had a drug issue, sometimes he drank a little too much alcohol; but he did not use drugs. Throughout the 10 years his case manager worked with him, she had met and seen plenty of his 'friends'- and these two had shown up out of no where a few months prior.

He lacked a strong support network- and human service agencies and the 'streets' are not enough. It can be a pretty painful reality to 'meet people where they are at.' And sometimes tracking down concerned family isn't even the whole issue.

The father of the first mentioned client, who had perished in his hallway for two weeks before being found, was finally contacted. When informed of what happened he said, "Oh, well what do you want me to do about it? Just donate whatever belongings he had to charity." And hung up the phone.

The common theme that anyone said about these guys was that they were nice and deserved more. In the case of the two deceased, when their needs were stabilized, they both functioned well and had always been able to maintain employment (however limited or sporadic opportunities were). When things got shaky, they struggled a bit; but always maintained their spirits of goodness. Same with the guy chastised for feeding birds. This especially makes their estrangements from family and society sad, because all three of them probably recognized the fact that most of the world had given up on them.

And I'm not trying to cast judgment on the families of estranged homeless 'vagrants.' I am trying to cast the humanity found in these individuals. I am sure these gentlemen put their family and loved ones through grief. But doesn't everybody? Everybody dishes some out and takes some- whether intentional or not. The majority of us flawed and complex human beings just want to be loved and accepted. And the environment for those surviving in the lowest depths of poverty is repulsive. Thank God there are people and agencies that go out of their way to channel some humane dignity (without judgment) to people who are living (alone) in the conditions of poverty.

The case manager, mentioned for the client found 'literally' dying in his bed, had not been an actual case manager for some time. But she had formed a connection with him; and decided to keep him- along with a tiny caseload of other people she knew it was in their best interest to remain as their 'worker.' Again, it ain't the type of biz where transferring people to a '20 something do gooder' to 'manage' their 'case' is a good idea. And I don't know who he would have been transferred to- but the point is that establishing real connections with people is a more beneficial consistency in their lives than shuffling them around to various people to apply specific techniques. She was the only person, during the last decade of his life that consistently knew who he was and where he came from- and that is probably why he identified her as the 'responsible' party for any future medical decisions he couldn't make on his own.

If you're wondering how she was doing during all of this, I can tell you as good as any one can that bore the whole load of someone's dignity. I remember when my grandfather was dying of cancer. There was enough money in our family to have his hospice occur in my grandparent's living room. Family was there 24/7 for those last few weeks in his life. His wife, his children, their current and former spouses, and his grandchildren spent a lot of time in that living room together. Some even flew in from out of town. While a constant flow of friends stopped by bringing food and comfort to all of us while he was in and out of coherence- and he knew we were all there. It was after this experience that I realized how convoluted death is, but that the buried silver lining is the power it has in bringing people together.

Everyone knows the sorrow and grief involved in losing a close loved one. Imagine witnessing someone not having the same fabric of loss to console them in their last moments of life. And then imagine being chosen by that person to be their fabric of loss. That's a tough pill to swallow, even if you are paid to do it.

It was hard to track down his family, between disconnected phone numbers and different addresses- his case manager left a note in the mailbox of 'possible' kin on a Wednesday night, and his brother called the next morning. Many family members gathered and surrounded him until he passed on the following Monday. They all watched the Packers play the Bears together, as he was in and out of coherence, because he loved watching football. He died in the arms of his sisters- one stroking his hair and the other petting his eyebrows. They said he looked serene and peaceful as he gasped his last breath.

I went to the memorial service. There were 9 of us that worked within the city's shelter network (or industry). Another 'shelter' client, or longtime friend, that the memorialized had requested to come to his bedside was also there. The rest of the room was filled with his family. There were two pictures and an urn in the front of the room. In one picture he looked to be in his 20's holding a trophy and smiling. In the other he was an infant on his mom's lap surrounded by his siblings.

One of his sisters greeted us upon our arrival. She provided a description of everyone in the picture, and thanked us for knowing her brother (I decided not to elaborate on the fact I only knew 'of' him- literally by name). She continued talking about how special her brother was to everyone, and shared a few childhood memories. I found a seat by his case manager as his other sister got up to describe the order of events. First, each sibling would get up and speak, then other family members, and then anyone else. She encouraged anyone who knew him in the past 10 years to speak- so that his family could live vicariously through them.

The common theme his family shared was that he had a great sense of humor, was amazing at sports, loved to dance, and had incredible charm with the ladies- everyone talked about his alluring 'swagger.'

Everyone also spoke of his kindness and generosity, and gave examples of how he inspired them. He had 6 siblings (two sisters and four brothers). His youngest brother wrote the following poem:

Confessions of a Bound Soul

Brother, my brother
How selfish was I
While you seemed to struggle
I sat idly by waiting

Brother, my brother
Yes, try as I might
I now realize
It was also my fight

Brother, my brother
Now look at your leg
There's so much left missing
Yet, not once did you beg

Brother, dear brother
Listen when I say
I will stick by your side
Until our final day.

The deceased had moved to the Twin Cities area for work. Somewhere along that journey he became disenchanted with the sporadic job opportunities, and possibly took more of an interest in drinking. It was around this time that he was described as 'entering' the shelter system- and the world of homelessness. It was very obvious that his family always loved him. They said in the beginning, of his 10 years on the streets, they reconnected with him at least once a year.

He was plagued with a great deal of shame, and did not want to ask for help or be a burden. His nephews recalled meeting him once and enjoyed a game of basketball. He never came around or reached out to his family after his mother died. They filed a missing persons report, but the police said there was little they could do in helping a grown person find his way back to his family. No one in his family had seen or heard from him in the past 4 or 5 years. They said they constantly prayed and missed him, and listened with both admiration and sadness as shelter staff spoke of him. Again, his generosity, sense of humor, and 'swagger' were elements reinforced. As well as how he was always respectful- and frequently spoke of his family...

There was not a dry eye in the crowded room when the service ended. His siblings came over to a few of us staff to thank us for being in his life. They explained how awful they felt about being estranged,

84

and told us how and when they tried to reach him. They also expressed how thankful they were that we found them- so that they could be with him at the end. They believe he held on so that they all could be reunited. They kept telling us that they were a tight family that loved him, we certainly believed them; but they really wanted to make sure we knew.

When the name of one of the squatters was brought up, the friend of the deceased spoke up for the first time- he said "oh"- and then shook his head while lowering his gaze back into his lap. He mentioned later that they quit hanging out around the time this mentioned squatter entered his life as a 'friend'- it was around the same time they were housed on opposite ends of the city, so it was hard to keep in contact.

The next day, my office mate, who had been to other memorial services for deceased 'clients'- said that this was the first time he saw such a big and loving family. He said all the other memorial services were small and comprised mostly of staff- not family. I guess this man can be considered one of the lucky ones.

Chapter Six

Said What You Mean
As performed by Railroad Earth

The existence of modern day homelessness is a societal issue that reflects our country's marriage to capitalism, an economic system that's manifestation is directly related to the practices of genocide and slavery (carried out post Columbus 'encounter').   Therefore, since capitalism is rooted in a racially based caste system that rewards individuals with economic gain, it is quite reasonable to consider poverty to be its direct inverse. Which makes the existence of people living in the conditions of poverty to be an intended consequence of a system- not biology.

Poverty can generally be understood as a person's limited economic access to acquiring basic needs like food and housing. All sorts of variables are attributed to 'causing' poverty, and genetics, or biology, is scientifically proven to not be a factor. So why are so many non-white (and white) populations subject to living it? And how come it can be so cyclical and generational? Seriously, no one individually wishes for people, especially people they don't even know, to be burdened with a life of hardship- yet it is a reality we must face because people living in the conditions poverty are now an institutionalized 'class' of people. The way we choose to collectively understand and address modern day homelessness is a testament to the will of the people against the power of greed.

In my opinion, the crowning achievement of the United States of America is how it is designed to be adaptive- and rooted in principles that ensure the 'people' are always steering the ship, so as to not be overturn and sunk by aristocracy. The decisions of how it operates and conducts itself are based on the belief that the 'elected' officials carrying out these functions reflect the will of its people.

We are currently fending off a brigade of corporate interests that have turned this country inside out with unrelenting aristocratic tactics and imperatives. Money and religion are not supposed to steer the wheel of a true democracy- yet they play instrumental roles in how policy is established and understood- oh how far we have come from the 'celebrated' spirit of our founding fathers- yet not too surprising when one considers how their 'vision' of equality; that aspired to give everyone the inalienable rights to life, liberty and the pursuit of happiness, was copulated with practices of racist genocide and slavery. Eventually those practices became 'illegal' and are a fact of history... and perhaps the living reality of homelessness will meet the same fate.

Freeing people, from being subject to oppressive conditions, does not systemically create an equal playing field when they are still restricted from acquiring the same type of economic gains and benefits that their exploitations provided. I don't believe that my great-great-great-great-great-great-great-great-great-great grandfather Anthony Day, who set foot on this land in the 17th century (as an indentured servant from England), individually proliferated genocide or slavery anymore than I believe that my purchase of a sweat shop factory t-shirt made in China means I individually support oppressive labor practices.

My ancestor was allowed to be 'free' and 'purchase' land after finishing his 7 year servitude obligation, and I live in a country with labor laws guaranteeing employers will provide a minimum wage and certain working conditions. Whereas the American Indians and African Americans, subject to genocide and slavery, were not allowed the same rights as white Europeans- similarly the tired hands and eyes working in

China do not receive comparable pay, and work in less desirable conditions, than the people performing the same type of labor in this country.

It is systemic practices that turn our individual beliefs and behaviors into the pragmatic actions that collectively perpetuate economic injustice. I did not personally earn this position on the socioeconomic spectrum anymore than children do when born into the conditions of poverty- whether white or non- white. That is where my feelings of helplessness reside. How to correct a wrong that is so heavily entrenched into a system while making sure all our societal trains 'run on time.' That is, how do we change an economic system built on racism? 'Socioeconomic' is a modern day telescope, if you will, that denotes the residuals of our country's utilization of blatant racism to establish its wealth.

It is very difficult to discuss how the historical racist policies shape the placement of people in relation to poverty. It seems that 'white' people struggle more than non-white in recognizing this issue. The best metaphor to describe this paradox is amnesia. And the most chilling antidote to make everyone wake up is the fact that you never know when the net may cast itself over you- and your race. Racism is merely a tool for exploitation- in its 'purest' form. Genocide and slavery were not new forms of exploitation 'tried' out over here, but using 'race' as the means to justify and administer their use was. And although a thorough analysis of our country's history, in relation to the development of its government and economy, sheds some light into the complexity involved in unraveling its past- it does not answer why we permit its unjust foundation to remain.

The workers 'rights' that have always existed in my lifetime are because of the courageous people that fought and sacrificed for them in the past- which would not have happened if 'people' didn't migrate to this land- whether freeing oppressive conditions holding them captive in their homelands or forced to be held captive in these lands.

This monumental migration also stripped all the rights from people living in this land- holding them captive in their homelands. These initial geographic reconfigurations have respectively morphed and continue obstructing people's path toward economic opportunity because of their race. And were echoed with 19th century government sponsored exclusionary immigration policies that were designed to attract Asian men for their labor, but not for their culture or families. Which is reminiscent to the way we currently tempt a 'poor' Latino working class to not only come and perform jobs for little pay and excessive hours- but to do it 'illegally.'

There is one common thread about exploitive practices in the United States, and that is money.

Someone, or some entity, always makes a profit from it, and we have a rich history of workers from all walks of life banding together in order to bring about better 'rights' for everyone. Overtime, efforts of solidarity influenced the government and private business interests to establish a 20th century middle class- and there is a sliver lining beyond its immediate effect of segregated neighborhoods. Yes, plenty of unequal access to quality public and private goods and services persist on the basis of skin tone- and 'whites' are systemically designed to prosper. But at the same time, there is now a path paved to redistribute wealth and power from a concentrated system to more of its people.

I find optimism in my belief that the 'white' children I grew up with will not allow systemic racism to continue into the future. It is quite startling to visit a family receiving public assistance, regardless of race, and imagine the 'childhood' the children are subject to by residing in 'low-income' neighborhoods (i.e., limited access to 'good' schools, blocks riddled with broken windowed homes and vacant business buildings, few backyards to freely play in, etc...)- and then to visit my niece and nephew the same day, in my sister and brother in law's boisterous and 'higher income' neighborhood- and compare the childhood they are subject to- with 'access' to much more privileged basic needs as they run around foot loose and fancy free in lush backyards.

It is unfair, and I'm hoping that the reason we let it permit is because we are collectively blinded by all the culturally created demands and distractions in life. It is also difficult to properly delineate who is responsible for 'what'- and 'what' is owed to who- because the historical narrative has created a subtle divide and conquer rift among the 'races'- or people.

How does one reverse white flight? Or the flight of non-white households seizing opportunity, and *also* leaving the 'crumbling' city neighborhoods for the more affluent suburban ones? What is the societal cost for those left behind? How does one go about untangling such an entrenched web? And why does the implicit racism that conceived this disparity get lost in translation? It seems as if we now hold individual people accountable for circumstances that are more reflective of what society has done rather than their own doing- we have lost any sense of collective empathy in understanding the plight of people.

Where do newly arrived 'poor' immigrant populations reside? How are the refugees, arriving from places in the world where our hands are in the cookie jar, doing? If public assistance programs aren't reducing the conditions of poverty for U.S. born citizens, what impacts do you think they have on people who not only lack English speaking abilities, but also come from lands not as fast paced and developed- having just vacated war torn and/or extremely 'improvised' countries. Culture shock, maybe? Oh, and how is current life on the reservations we forced to exist?

If we are part of the white majority and doing well (having 'worked' hard or not) are we supposed to say "fuck it"- their problem, not mine. Do we reduce the serious disgrace of a human injustice systemically percolating for 500 years to a bunch of thugs, slow drivers and greedy casino owners; and instead worry about which celebrity wore some overpriced piece of shit better than someone else? In this complex and 'post racial' society, an urgency in properly acknowledging systemic racism is essential in eradicating poverty so that all childhoods are less affected by income inequality.

Race is a social construct, poverty is an environment - and societal influences impact our perceived correlations between race and poverty. In the United States, race and poverty are also muddled with the concept of crime.

To clarify overlapping terminology, poverty is a condition that people have been living in for centuries. The foundation of this country created a system to specifically place non-white populations in conditions of poverty. These conditions were more 'impoverished' than those of whites also living in conditions of poverty. Overtime, the practice of specifically placing non-whites in more impoverished conditions was stopped, but compensating, or systemically placing both groups in better positions, to access wealth has not occurred. Rags to riches stories cross all color lines, but even playing fields in opportunity do not. Historically, we, as a country, have always provided whites with more economic upward mobility opportunities than non-whites.

"Homelessness" captures the water level of both white and non-white populations living in the conditions of poverty. Some of the people do live without places to reside, while others are housed in safe settings. It is more an indication of financial stability, or income inequality. In addition, people of all races can and do move in and out of poverty. The lingering remnant of racism is discerned by the fact that many of the people remaining submerged (or generationally living in conditions of poverty) are from communities of color.

We are now living in what can be termed as a post Civil Rights era racial society. Or 'post racial', which denotes a time when the government no longer engages in overt systemic racist practices. We must always remember that race is inherently distinct from poverty; while recognizing how the impact of policies overtime makes them appear to no longer be mutually exclusive. Poverty, like wealth, is a dynamic condition that seems to become a more static condition for people of certain decent... and in the case of poverty, when convicted of crimes.

According to the Sentencing Project, the United State's current incarcerated population is 2.2 million people. That is a 500% increase from the 100,000 to 200,000 incarcerated population averages- maintained from the 1920's until the 1970's 'War on Drugs' policies. A heart wrenching fact when you truly consider the amount of time in relation to the increase in numbers. And even worse, about 60% of the 2.2 million people incarcerated are from communities of color. And roughly a quarter of the 2.2 million people are serving time for non-violent drug offenses. What is going on?

The burgeoning private prison industry ought to receive and draw the same amount of criticism and scrutiny as private military defense contractors like Blackwater Security and its ilk- but it doesn't. These companies (and public government-run prisons) are getting an amazing discount on a tremendous amount of labor. And part of the difference, in societal attention, could easily be attributed to the way we regard the voices and rights of 'prisoners' versus 'military personal.' I'm not trying to place more regard for one over the other, but simply pointing out that we literally lock up and throw away the key to the lives of those convicted as being on the wrong side of the law- and that such complacency to the status quo is causing great exploitation and devastation in different areas of our society. Status quo, of course, is referring to the existing socioeconomic spectrum.

The empirical research demonstrating how childhood poverty greatly affects the likelihood that a person will engage in criminal activities is well known. And pointing out the discrepancy between sentencing guidelines for the exact same amount of the exact same drug (albeit in different forms) is a disparaging example of the subjective nature of law.

Powder form cocaine is more prevalent among the more affluent members of society- while freebase form, or crack, is more prevalent among the less affluent. And since the demographic breakdown between more and less affluent 'neighborhoods' reflects racially based housing policies of the past- then is it really a coincidence that we discriminate over which one is more permissible? And what effect does the lack of career opportunities, due to low educational attainments, have on the likelihood a person will engage in the business of the illegal drug trade? And what impact does not having 'affluent' money for legal counsel, after being charged with economic or controlled substance crimes- have on conviction rates?

96

And really, what other opportunities (besides winning the lottery or becoming a professional athlete or a 'rapper') do these children have to aspire to? That is not a joke- it is a truth in numbers, not ability. A sad reality that we as a society need to change- not by 'trying' to make people better, but by truly making opportunities to achieve financial stability more equal.

For instance, the financially strapped 'free' public schools in lower income neighborhoods are providing a different quality of education than the more financially robust and resource abundant private and public schools in higher income neighborhoods. The result of this difference is that an astoundingly higher percentage of the student body is graduating from schools of the latter than the former- which influences the career aspirations, and opportunities, for the children brought up in each respective school system. That is not an equal opportunity. And what is causing these drastically different outcomes? The schools, the children, the teachers- or something else...

This statistically significant occurrence is referred to as the achievement gap. The truth of the matter is that no one knows what to do or how to go about properly addressing it. It is not a phenomenon that is easy to track or closely monitor.

Because quite honestly, how does one accurately 'view' this problem? Do we break it down by income?

Will basing a school's student body receiving reduced lunches best capture that? What about race? Is it a non-white concern or are whites struggling too? Is there a difference between newly arrived Asian American children and children of 3rd generation Asian American parents? Is it an urban or rural problem? And what effect does English speaking ability have--- and how do we measure a child's progress?

You would need various maps to try capturing 'all of those' variables, and still have to figure out how to actually measure it. The best 'variable' to measure a composite picture is to use state wide standardized test scores. These tests cover different subjects (i.e., math, science, and reading), and are administered during specific grade levels. But this composite picture can really only quantify how the student body of a 'school' or 'district' tests, not an individual child- and only during certain grade levels (i.e., 3rd, 8th, and 11th grades)- which almost assumes a child's learning environment is constant (i.e., teachers, textbooks, home life, etc...). It also cannot account for any changes caused by switching districts, schools, or classrooms- so there is no way to follow individual student progressions in relation to their comprehension of concepts.

Let's say child A had little English speaking ability in 3rd grade and did not pass the reading test. She makes amazing progress in her English speaking abilities by the 8th grade, and has tremendous personal improvement on the reading test. If the score is 'below' the passable level, it is still considered a 'failure.' Those failures negatively affect the already compromised (compared to the more affluent and higher test score producing schools) funding- causing less capacity for the school to adequately address the situation. Imagine the 'aggregate' impact that unequally prepared children have on their schools and districts. Is that really fair- and is it really 'anyone's' fault?

Obviously, the correlations between race and poverty make it a complex problem to properly gauge. And the recent implementation of "No Child Left Behind" policies- financially reprimanding schools instead of ensuring adequate funding is provided to improve them- make it an alarming concern because of the long-term societal impacts these policies will create.

The positive impacts that early childhood education has on a child's academic performance are undeniable, and I truly wonder why our societal efforts focus on 'determining' negative outcomes instead of facilitating positive ones. Especially since the schools with noticeable educational gaps, and receiving negative policy consequences, are overrepresented by non-white, lower-income, and non-English speaking populations. From my 'jaded' perch, it almost seems like the complacency in the continuation of these policies deprives children of equal opportunities.

I've faced my own achievement gap. In 8th grade I took higher algebra, but decided to take lower level classes throughout high school. I was required to take non-credit earning remedial courses to get into college. It was not until grad school that I finally understood the basic linear relationship between exponents and curves on graphs. I felt like I was 'working' double time (and I think I was compared to my peers)- because I had to take extra time to make sure I finally understood the basic concepts so I could fully comprehend the advanced ones.

Not to mention the 'Excel' learning curve. My 7th grade keyboard classes were literally on typewriters. I submitted a handful of computer-processed papers in high school, and did not even know what Excel 'was' until 2004 (and rarely had to open up a spreadsheet). Another prerequisite for this grad school program was to be competent and proficient in Excel. I hurt my brain, and relied on the kindness of my classmates, to slowly get me up to snuff. I am now so intimately acquainted with Excel that I don't know if it is a good or bad thing.

As excruciating as the grad school experience was, I am happy I did it, and know that I am no dummy- and neither is anyone else. But I overcame this gap 'late' in my academic adventures, after I already gained intellectual confidence. So in terms of achievement, the gap I faced was due to nothing more

100

than me being lazy and unprepared. While the gap many other people face is due to an unfair societal playing field they are subject to early in life that limits their opportunity in being prepared- that was (and still is) created by historical and recent policy decisions that exacerbate the gap people have in accessing quality education.

Which brings me to another point in the correlations made between poverty, race, and crime. Is the thrill seeking shoplifting, that my white girlfriends and I engaged in, easier to do because the consequence of 'getting caught' is decreased by the misguided concern of preventing non-white people (who appear) to have an actual need in engaging in such behavior? A definitive answer to that is impossible.

As are many other questions related to muddled convergence of race, poverty and crime. I believe the disposition for anyone to learn or commit crimes is relatively the same- but I think our collective understanding becomes punitive when the measured engagement in these 'activities' (educational attainments and criminal behavior), is used to indicate where people 'end up'- instead of being proactively used to show where they 'start out.'

Now a little dose of actual responsibility, in earning my own money to cover my basic needs, curbed any 'temptation' or desire to 'stimulate' any of my free time with shoplifting. My first dabble in 'stealing' was age 8 with a Hershey bar at a grocery store. My dad immediately brought me back to the store, upon noticing my deed, and I both returned the candy bar and apologized for my behavior to the store manager. The next escapade was the two little shopping sprees with my gal pals around the age 11 or 12, and although my fingers didn't do the actual lifting, my conscience caught up with me too quickly to turn into a habit.

Plus, some of the lifters were getting 'caught' and punished. Same with a couple of flirtations with the cash register till at one of the places I worked at during high school. These 'flirtations' were also very limited- and covered the cost of a pizza to chomp down during a shift. Regardless, for whatever reason, I had the inclination to commit crimes and was able to rehabilitate my ways before heading down a destructive path of havoc and so forth.

We often think about giving people second chances, but our societal actions seem complacent to the status quo. And the status quo, in my opinion, operates in a manner that reinforces the socioeconomic spectrum without giving people fair first chances- which further erodes our collective societal quality of life by also restricting people from having second chances. I do not think that people are any less capable than myself; regardless if they fall into any combination of the following: born into poverty, are of a certain race, or convicted of a crime. So we all ought to be gravely concerned about the over representation of all people who obtain low educational attainments- as well as all the people that live in our incarceration system.

And using a serial killer, or some other heinous crime, example to diffuse the reality of the 'preventable' crimes we are locking up an astonishing amount of people for does not do anyone justice. We need to look at the facts and patterns of what we collectively do- not split hairs on 'hyperbole' to justify the decision to remain complacent.

I am guessing that most people do not base where to service their car on whether the person below the hoist has been convicted of a crime, yet the car shop does. Landlords have a similar weight in influencing where people can be housed. The common practice of employers not hiring ex-felons makes it difficult for a staggering amount of willing and able adults, charged with non-violent crimes, to prosper.

Furthermore, many members in low income communities are met with similar obstacles in working their way out of poverty, because of the lower income levels and educational attainments related to being brought up in the conditions of poverty. According to the Wilder Research 2009 Minnesota Homeless study, children and their families are the fastest growing segment of the homeless. If we do not drastically slow down this growth, we can expect a similar increase in the ever-growing incarcerated population.

I was born into a place on the socioeconomic spectrum with an abundance of opportunity to pursue my life's ambitions from the get go, and this position has enough buoyancy to catapult back into it from any second chance I may find myself in. This is not bragging or complaining, but merely stating the truth. This does not, however, prevent me from suffering or struggling to figure what is expected of me.

I've been in some 'dark' personal places and have been overwhelmed by the demands of life. And so it is really a sense of duty, not guilt or pity that motivates me to continue fighting in the elusive battle of systemic racism and economic injustice.

I entered the non-profit world pounding the actual pavement in the trenches of poverty, and I suddenly realized that I was in a place so far removed from that. To me, I had become a paid spectator to the theatre I wanted to help change. And paid spectator hardly denotes the fast paced and integrated program involvement of many administrative and upper management non-profit positions. But it was time for me to make a dash.

As I sat in front of the computer for 90% of my workdays, I fantasized about side projects and relished any time spent with front line staff- when we would brain storm solutions to operating strategies reliant on contractual policy procedures. The parting of ways with my employer was abrupt, but not surprising. Bridges were not burned, but paths were parted. It has been the furthest experience of 'ease' in my life; I lived off of a severance package for a bit, received some unemployment benefits for a spell- and am now living off of the nest egg of retirement savings that I was doing a pretty good job of growing.

There is one sobering reality that frustrates me more than any stressful day at work ever could. Our society is structured around a system that allows people with no personal investment or real community interest, in low-income neighborhoods, to have more control of these neighborhoods than the people actually living in them. And since affluent neighborhoods do not face this same indirect form of discrimination, you can rest assure that it is a circumstance of the lingering racial caste system that our country has been built around.

If it is known that growing up in the conditions of poverty increases one's likelihood to engage in criminal behavior, and former inmates are not allowed back into these neighborhoods- where exactly, as a society, do we expect them to go? They certainly are not welcomed into the more affluent ones, so really, what is our collective expectation in actual rehabilitation?

At the same time, I would argue that almost no one is happy with the 'state' of our nation's public assistance programs. Unfortunately, too much attention (which somehow transforms to credence) is given to people who are far removed from it and are over critical of the miniscule latitude in spending decisions recipients make. Currently, most public employment and housing assistance programs are intended to eradicate the conditions of poverty by improving one's access to stabilizing a need. This individual based structure does not encourage the people living in conditions of poverty to change it, which may contribute to the cyclical and concentrated nature of it.

The majority of government assistance programs stem from federal level, and each state and their localities are given some leeway in how they are administered. I am privy to many of the federal regulations, as well as Minnesota's unique commitment and investment in improving the lives that are living in the conditions of poverty. This commitment is formed by various private and public entities. For better or for worse, this crazy platform gave me an opportunity to envision a realistic win-win strategy for everyone. And do you know what is most quintessential about it? There is not a trace of race in it (figuratively speaking).

106

That is why I am not done fantasizing about ways to adjust existing public funding to actually empower people, residing in lower income neighborhoods, to become the stewards of their own communities. Which in turn, will reduce the racial recidivism of people living in the conditions of poverty, because poverty in itself will be decreased.

.

Chapter Seven

For the Good Times
As performed by Al Green

Combating poverty, which will help dismantle systemic racism, is so simple that it must be impossible. Let's pretend I am as naïve as I was in that middle school gymnasium, but with my adult cognitive skills to ask 'why?' There are so many societal contradictions that seem 'right.' Or there are living realities that are allowed to carry on and be contested as if they are matters of 'preference' in our society... rather than the consequences of financial or political initiatives that are logically 'wrong.'

Evidently 'gays' can be together, yet states are trying to make it 'illegal' for them to marry. McDonald's top selling menu items are soft drinks and highly caloric 'burgers'- yet it is a proud and major sponsor of the

Olympics. And most people won't even 'drive through' neighborhoods with high poverty rates, yet the majority of people that actually live in (and have difficultly in being able to literally 'drive out' of) them are not in any financial or political positions- to oversee and effectively change- the conditions in which they live...

In the case of same sex marriage, one can build a grassroots campaign (or excessively fund organizations) to canvass the political airwaves with propaganda and fear mongering techniques to create an atmosphere where **the idea** *that the marriage of two people of the same sex is not 'equal' to the marriage of two people of the opposite sex* **is made debatable**. I cannot, for the life of me, figure out what 'benefit' the promoters of this culture war are trying to gain in their mission to exclude same sex couples from 'mainstream' society.

The case of McDonald's and the Olympics is a little more cut and dry- money. The high ranking religious leaders and elected officials are not necessary to carry any of the banners for this campaign. McDonald's shells out the dough to advertise, and the Olympics is properly funded. Interesting how no one, not even for a millisecond, believes that the strong and lean athletes snarf down value meals before their big events.

And in the case of people living in the conditions of poverty while not having the financial or political clout to change the 'actual' conditions in which they live? Like in the case of 'criminalizing' same sex marriage, we are desensitized on the real merits for conversations because propaganda and fear mongering strategies dilute the airwaves with volatile 'issues' to debate. But unlike same sex marriage, and more like the profit earning motivation of McDonald's- disenfranchising people living in the conditions of poverty creates an ill-gotten economic gain (and that sentence is not accusing, or even suggesting, that McDonald's disenfranchises people- it is merely pointing out that its interest in the Olympics is financial).

Disenfranchising people does not necessarily increase wealth unless the disenfranchised are being exploited. That is where I am at a loss with the same sex marriage debate- all the bigotry and hate is not creating an increase in anyone's pocketbook- I guess I'll never understand it and will get back on topic. Hence, I can more easily see how the untapped supply and demand mechanics that paralyzes the affected populations, living in the conditions of poverty, also polarizes their circumstance by shaping the way 'kitchen table' conversations are played out in societal public and political arenas.

I will use North Minneapolis, one of my state's more 'renowned' high poverty areas, as an example. The untapped supply side of that neighborhood's economy is its residents. The men and women with criminal backgrounds are a major supply segment that is not able to work- or they are very limited in the number of employers willing to hire them (Which is so erroneous and crazy since many of the same employers have no problem using and exploiting their labor when they are locked up! UGH!) At the same time; its other residents, without criminal backgrounds, are untapped resources for both the supply and demand sides of their neighborhoods- simply because they are short changed by opportunity- and plagued with having less 'credible' credentials in being the organizing force to demand the wants and desires of their neighborhood.

And while both of these neighborhood constituents groups are being 'ignored' (or financially and politically paralyzed)- the rest of the metropolitan area is flogged with stories and news reports of shootings, robberies, vandalisms, and any 'other' undesirable acts- as being normal and everyday occurrences in this neighborhood, which makes them politically polarized from their more affluent (or financially solvent) metro area 'neighborhood' neighbors. It is polarizing because the narrative being delivered suggests that high poverty neighborhoods are so bad that no one should give a shit... almost along the lines of "give em enough rope and they'll hang themselves" – or more like, the poverty is so prevalent, and too many of the residents are so far gone, that one would literally be risking their life getting involved in any of the concerns in the neighborhood.

I find this paralysis and polarization of my community members to be unwarranted. Or, I do not #1 believe that people residing in low income (or high poverty, however you want to slice it) neighborhoods are 'bad' and undeserving of opportunities to make a living with wages much higher than the minimum wage or poverty level guidelines. And #2, I am not scared of North Minneapolis- never had been, never will be. I have done a lot of 'home visits' in various low income neighborhoods in my day- all over the Twin Cities. I even took a tour of the San Francisco 'Tenderloin' area... and 'fear' is not a word that would remotely describe my feelings of 'low income' neighborhoods- pissed off and disgusted with what we allow in our society would be a more accurate description.

I speak of North Minneapolis because I live across the river from it, and 'travel through'- and visit it- for non-work related activities. What I've seen and experienced is a neighborhood, and its people, systemically restricted from civic participation. It is a neighborhood with a low median income that does not attract businesses to it. And its housing 'landscape' is filled with properties owned by many landlords that fall into two categories. One type tries to deter crime with strict rental eligibility criterion and the other tries to make a buck by providing absolutely no oversight or maintenance of its units (i.e., slumlords).

It is a neighborhood where businesses decide if and where it will locate and landlords determine where people can live. So what rights do the people really have? People are perfectly capable of preparing themselves (and their communities) for life without benefits, which in turn increases the vitality of the neighborhood for everyone. Isn't that part of some econ 101 theory? The people earning money by making widgets will bring their paychecks back into local economy (i.e., buying food, clothing, cars, etc...).

So why aren't people residing in the conditions of poverty doing it? Well, the educational playing field they start out in is the first possible contributing factor, but so is the lack of livable wage jobs and affordable housing options- so they never get the chance to use widget earning paychecks to pay their rent... or to put back into their local economy.

A lot of the residents in these neighborhoods receive public employment, housing, and other income assistance to stabilize their individual basic needs. The individualized administration structure of receiving these services limits their individual ability to stabilize their community needs. Or, signing up for public assistance is not like joining a gardening or scrap booking club in affluent neighborhoods- where you suddenly have access to a whole network of people with similar 'free' time, financial stability, and passion for problem solving issues involving troublesome weeds or faulty cricuts.

We all love our privacy, don't we? There are very intricate details collected that are related to personal trials and tribulations when signing up for public assistance, and this creates a 'barrier' in them being able to help each other. Now I'm not contesting the richness or intention of data collection. Or comparing the knowledge of who owns a $100 garden tool to that of a person receiving some type of monthly assistance- the 'need' reflected in signing up for each type of respective network or service already speaks volume (i.e., hobby versus survival). But why are the hobby enthusiasts more at liberty to easily help one another? They may have criminal backgrounds, and other 'personal' information, that is not aired out to their fellow gardeners and scrap bookers.

It makes sense that laws are in place restricting how information is shared for public assistance recipients. But the consequence of this is that service providers are challenged in facilitating the development of any voluntary transportation, childcare, or networking cooperatives amongst people living in the conditions of poverty. Things 'needed' before they are able to join expensive 'hobby' groups. At the agency I worked, we had various volunteer and supported work positions that participants could do in order to meet their mandated participation hours. This was great, and although they were able to manage and produce monthly newsletters, they were not allowed to address or mail them out because of confidentiality issues.

Similarly, as staff, we knew the single and family households from both housing and employment programs. We knew who was living where and what possible benefits various people could have in helping each other. Person A is in a housing program and lives here. She is unable to work but can definitely watch children in a pinch- and her 18-year old son has a car and drivers license. Person B is in an employment program and lives in the same neighborhood, in fact, only two doors down from Person A. They do not formally know each other and are rarely in the office at the same time. Person B has a great paying job in the suburbs, but sometimes seems 'unreliable.' His 2-year-old daughter needs extra medical attention from time to time, and he currently relies on someone else to drive him to and from work everyday. Wouldn't it be great to introduce these two, person A and person B, to see if they could figure out a way to help each other in times of need?

I'm not suggesting some breach of sensitive information, or letting personal information float around about any person who has ever received public assistance. Information regarding any time spent in treatment, being convicted of a crime, receiving formal evictions, or any other personal information that is their business- should remain 'their' business. And I'm glad privacy laws are in place. I'm talking about contact information and descriptions of any help they need or assistance they are willing to provide to their community- and giving them the latitude to administer the use of such information.

I will draw one more comparison of my privileged life to show how we, as humans, are bound to sometimes feel frustratingly helpless because of circumstance. It will also illuminate how a cooperative network could be so beneficial for many of the households, living in the conditions of poverty, that are headed by single adults. I was once married, now I am not. For 6 years, we were both stewards of a house we owned together. I've been the sole steward (or single head of household) of the house for the past 2.5 years.

As shared stewards (or two people concerned about the same household), and things like an insurance company demanding the roof be replaced- we figured out this unintended expense together. When mice and other pesky rodents roamed around, I sent the husband to take care of it. If my payday was two days out, dinner was on him. It's not that we were ever 'flush'- but we had each other to rely on, which made the day-to-day struggles a lot more bearable.

Like if he went to start his car at 5 in the morning, and it wouldn't start- my 'late' 8 o'clock work start time could accommodate driving him to and from work before we had to even think about dealing with the repair. Things have not been as 'smooth' for me being the sole steward of the household in the past 2.5 years.

I certainly can't 'cover' the same costs (as before) by myself, but I do have possible 'means' outside of applying for public assistance- and they are not big ego boosters. For example; when I had to come up with over $2,000 to sell the 2009 Honda Civic back to the dealership in the summer of 2010, in order to not have ongoing payments I couldn't afford- I had to bow my head, tuck my tail firmly between my legs, and cross my fingers as I asked my grandmother for the money. She gave it to me without question- and my brother was able to give me his paid off 'used' car.

When I miscalculated and needed at least $600 to cover first of the month expenses a couple months ago, I had to buck up and shamefully ask my parents to borrow it to me… after receiving so much of their money 'in times of need' during the past year (I paid them back promptly, by the way).

When I came home to a squirrel prancing around in the living room, I ran outside sobbing and called my mom. I needed to talk to somebody who could calm me down enough to get the caged dog out of harms way. I relied on my neighbor, a co-worker, and my dad to make sure the critter was out of the house. And my generous (and handy) brother in law came over, after working all day, and worked past sundown fixing the hole in the chimney. (I have not put the dog in a kennel since, both for his safety and so that he can fend off any intruding buggers).

If I'm 'dying' to have a dinner besides the egg or frugally simple diet I am now accustomed, I casually call my parents and ask what they are up to that night. When I have car problems, I panic! First, there is the getting to my obligations, and second- how the Hell can I afford ANY type of repair? I'm so spoiled that I've never relied on the bus line, and figuring out routes to fit my immediate needs is a task in itself.

Plus, I am not used to asking for help for what is essentially my own responsibility- even though circumstances 'out of my control' put me in the situation I am in. I accept blame for what I can, but also learn and grow from my mistakes. For instance, it would seem that I should just 'get rid of the house'... but right now is not a good time to put a house on the market- so my options are limited.

I did try renting it out and moved into an apartment. Not only because it is expensive, but also because I was sick of doing 'everything' by myself. Mowing the lawn, shoveling snow, dealing with ice dams, and other miscellaneous homeownership 'quirks' can be stressful. The lack of drainage in the basement makes me indifferent about much loved rainfalls (carrying a shop vac full of water up a flight of stairs to be poured outside sucks). But by renting an apartment (for the first time in years) I learned that the solace of privacy is priceless.

I have found new glory in cleaning out gutters and other house 'stuff' that used to bother me. Plus, I have put a lot of sweat equity into this place. I am happy that I have not added any debt to my credit cards (which are relatively small balances with 0% APR- and could easily be paid off once I'm 'hired' somewhere).

It is amazing how much I realize I do not 'need' that I always thought I did (i.e., picking up a $15 wall décor item for a bare wall while on a toilet paper run). And noticing that when I had a steady income, I was more inclined to 'charge' something- thinking I'd be able to pay it off in the future (i.e., airline ticket for some festive or fun future concert plans)- even though there was no indication that my actual income would increase. That silly urge, which I kept pretty reasonable, does not even exist anymore. If I ain't got the cash in hand, and I'm not willing to 'beg' for it, then I know I don't need it.

In the case of me sobbing over the squirrel, I am not scared of little animals or some overdramatic baby that cannot handle the small stuff. The squirrel incident was a little over a year into being the sole steward of the home. I was emotionally and financially stressed to a degree I'd never faced before. Upon seeing the creature- I knew that #1 squirrels can cause great expensive havoc and #2 that there must be some gaping hole or entry point for critters to get into the house, most likely another expensive fix.

What I didn't know was the extent of either of those. Hell, back in married life, I came home to the house completely ransacked by some economic opportunists. The abnormally pushed in gate was clue #1, the open side door was #2. When I noticed the laptop was missing from the desk in the entryway, I calmly called the husband- "did you happen to stop home and pick up the laptop?"

When he said "no" ... I didn't even flinch before storming into the house for the little doggie. Once I found him, and knew that he was 'okay'- I called the husband back to verify that we were indeed burglarized before calling the police. And the expense and loss from that monstrosity (and 'possible' danger) was much greater than the baby squirrel accidently falling down a

120

chimney. But I didn't have someone invested in the struggle with me as I did in the past- and it took a little while for me to define my new idea of stability. Which was relatively 'easy' for me, because I come from a family that has not experienced generational poverty (yet).

The notion of 'stability' is often cited as a positive outcome for public employment and housing assistance programs. The definition varies, and is based on the stated outcomes premised by service providers and approved by funders. I would love to see an option in the community drafted by the actual people trying to achieve it.

The federal Housing and Urban Development Housing Choice Voucher Program Section 8 is a large permanent rental assistance program. Most public housing authorities and programs administering these subsidies have incredibly long waiting lists, so they are 'hard' to get. But once a person 'receives' a voucher subsidy- they are usually able to keep it 'forever'- which ensures their long-term housing stability... as long as they remain within the locality it was issued and are not convicted of a felony crime. Yes, a criminal record is basis for both the denial and termination of this desperately needed rental assistance program.

As you can see, having a criminal background makes things 'doubly' hard in all income (or economic) areas of life that is already difficult when living in the conditions of poverty. Which makes it even tougher, to both find a place to live and a job to afford it, in the already tough employment and housing markets. An ex-felon also politically disenfranchised, as most states are unwilling to allow them to cast a vote. Being poor, and convicted of economic or controlled substance related crimes, most definitely fits the premise of exploiting the labors of a disenfranchised population (to me anyway). And since particular races and economic classes well over represent this disenfranchised population--- I'll leave it at that.

Now we can consider the disenfranchisement of ex-felons from society to be a cost they knowingly waged when committing a crime- or we can look more into it and assess if the actual crimes and time served are justifiable. OR, we can thoroughly reevaluate how our societal institutions and policies adversely affect, not only the attainment of upward economic mobility, but also the actualization of financial stabilization- for too many individuals living in the conditions of poverty.

And perhaps focusing attention on the circumstance of 'ex-felons' seems like the 'wrong' starting place in examining the situation, but like the aggressive retail clerks in shopping malls- it seems like many of the employers and landlords are racially profiling (or attempting to avoid) potential 'criminals' from being hired or housed by including petty and misdemeanor convictions as exclusion criterion- thus, restricting more individuals from achieving stability and expanding their economic opportunities.

And since this is such a daunting, longitudinal, and complex 'problem' that has many overlapping and impossible to properly decipher variables- we've got to figure out a way to immediately increase employment and housing opportunities that does not interfere with the already politically vulnerable public employment and housing assistance programs. An approach needs to be developed that focuses on empowering public assistance recipients while maintaining the existing administration structure of these essential services.

And I know it can be done in Minnesota. A marriage between its Minnesota Family Investment Program (MFIP) and Housing Trust (HTF) subsidy program is the magic recipe. The former is a public temporary employment assistance program for families, and the latter is a semi permanent rental assistance program. The first priority would be to address a couple MFIP specific policy 'quirks.'

The objective of any temporary public assistance program should focus more on preparing participants for life without benefits, instead of the vague notion of increasing self-sufficiency. Over the years, politically motivated legislative changes have drastically impacted both the amounts and types of service people receive from MFIP. Participants of this program are required to document a certain amount of hours engaged in predetermined activities to earn a modest monthly cash grant and qualify for additional assistance with childcare, transportation, education, clothing, training, and identification expenses specific to employment. There are two slight policy adjustments that could really benefit participants, and their communities, in the long term.

The first is related to the tightened regulations around education- adults are no longer encouraged to obtain their high school diploma or G.E.D. once they reach the age 19. This activity is no longer track-able, which means any time spent engaging in the activity does not count towards the mandated amount of hours a participant must complete each month in order to receive a full cash grant and other benefits. MFIP uses a sanction system to enforce participation, which withholds participants from receiving benefits- and an adult pursuing a high school level education should not be a cause for sanction. In fact, increasing education levels ought to be a priority.

The second policy adjustment has to do with transportation. As it stands now, the program will pay for any expenses related to obtaining proper identification (i.e., the 20 or so dollar fees to secure a birth certificate or social security card as well as actual state issued I.D. requiring such documentation). But it will only pay for driver's education courses, and the actual test, if one is employed at a job requiring them to drive a vehicle. The requisite ought to proactively allow anyone to have the expenses paid in obtaining a driver's license regardless of current employment status. The value in being able to drive is a common qualification for many potential job opportunities, and allowing participants to be prepared for such a requirement will increase their employability- and will decrease the 'illegal' driving incidents due to not having a valid driver's license.

These two little tweaks, in conjunction with a methodic facilitation in creating voluntary public assistance networks, could lead to a community building effort spearheaded by MFIP participants. The effort would focus on influencing both businesses and landlords to be more lenient with a person's 'criminal' past in determining what they are capable of doing today. The overall idea being that empowering one segment of the homeless population will have a trickle effect for everyone. It will also prepare them, and their communities, for a life without benefits; which will decrease the water level of people living in the conditions of poverty.

I have formulated two distinct, but interrelated, projects in the hopes of coordinating public employment and housing assistance services in a way that does not reinforce the socioeconomic spectrum in relation to poverty. The first is to develop a MFIP and rental assistance repository, which will provide a geographical map of the current long-term rental assistance subsidies in the state's two largest counties.

I did not thoroughly describe how a lot of rental assistance is distributed, but it is common practice to do so through a shelter system. Hence, the shelters have a magnetic effect of attracting people, when they are in a housing crisis, so that they can become eligible for subsidies. The idea of coordinating these programs is to create a path for working families to obtain rental assistance without having to physically enter a shelter, which has both high monetary and social costs. The social costs have longer negative effects when the disruption of school, childcare, and other essential day-to-day networks is considered.

The other purpose of the repository is related to the other project, which is the participant based community-building component. Information regarding landlords and the location of properties accepting rental assistance will be crucial in crafting neighborhoods

126

welcoming to individuals exiting the incarceration system.

This project would be comprised of ten MFIP participants receiving a Minnesota Housing Trust Fund (HTF) subsidy. An HTF subsidy is a long-term subsidy administered by the state that is very similar to the HUD Section 8 subsidies- without the criminal background restriction.

The subsidy is crucial because it will ensure participant housing needs are met while preparing them to be ready to enter the job market as they set the foundation to building their community. The 10 participants must be housed within close proximity of one another and to a central hub and office space required to carry out the project. The project must also have a car or van for the participants to use throughout the project.

The first six months of the project will be spent addressing the individual stabilization needs for each participant. These activities will include developing long-term career and housing transition plans, and facilitating household budget workshops to create 3-year plans for their expenses during the project. There are 10 positions that will be assigned to each participant based on their identified skills, desires, and input. The number in parenthesis denotes how many people are needed to fill for each project role:

> Business Canvasser and Negotiator (2)
> Childcare Dispatch (1)
> Landlord Canvasser and Negotiator (2)
> Neighborhood Canvasser and Negotiator (1)
> Newsletter Editor and Event Planner (1)
> Prison Canvasser and Negotiator (2)
> Transportation Dispatch (1)

The work schedule for each position will be 25 hours a week. It is imperative that these activities are considered track-able and in full compliance with the MFIP program.

The first six months will also be spent training them for their individual and collective roles for the remaining 2.5 years of project. The project will be presented as a task force, and will formally designate organizational roles and expectations. It will also establish a formal meeting schedule, agenda template, and communications format. It is desired that all participants will become experts in tenant rights and how they relate to rental assistance recipients.

The method used to assign them to their specific community engagement roles will be similar to how the neighborhood and prison canvassers will engage those job seeking populations in gathering their employment skills, desires, and input. The neighborhood canvasser will also be gathering the type of community needs residents wish to see in the neighborhood.

The business canvasser will survey the neighborhood for vacant and unused buildings in the area. The business and prison negotiators will use the potential employee and neighborhood needs information to broker a potential workforce, as well as a pool of future customers, with businesses. In exchange, they will negotiate for apprenticeships and job placements.

The childcare and transportation dispatches will compile and organize the voluntary needs and availability of the services neighbors are willing to contribute to the cooperatives. And the newsletter and event planner will engage community members to actively participate in the project- whether as a volunteer childcare provider, ride share member, or additional canvassers.

The childcare cooperative is essential for families receiving MFIP as much as it is for ones not. The benefit is huge in stabilizing employment, but there are a couple of 'living in the conditions of poverty' specific concerns that would be alleviated with a cooperative option.

The cost differentiation between childcare assistance obtained while receiving MFIP compared to the actual out of pocket expense is enormous. And accordingly, each participant is responsible for completing the proper paperwork so the county can verify the childcare provider legitimacy. They are also responsible for submitting the hours actually worked to be cross-referenced with what is billed to the county. Any inconsistency is carefully investigated and the participant is responsible for hours compensated that were not actually worked- and they are legally reprimanded with charges of fraud. Childcare providers are properly reprimanded for any inconsistencies on their behalf as well.

The justifiable strict oversight creates complications related to properly requesting childcare coverage for a workforce subject to sporadic employment engagements, inconsistent scheduling, irregular work hours, and last minute shift opportunities that are conditions propagated from the employers hiring them. This may have the adverse effect of participants turning down shifts, or not being able to work, because of coverage issues.

In addition, the steep economic 'drop off' from receiving to no longer receiving this benefit is not a big step toward self-sufficiency when the income is adjusted to reflect childcare assistance. And creating a cooperative network will provide more options for people to obtain childcare whether they are receiving MFIP or not.

The transportation ride share and carpool cooperative is essential in communities where its members rely on unreliable or public transportation. For instance, without a car, most people become accustomed to revolving around inflexible bus schedules and having to switch buses multiple times. Imagine how less stressful it would be to have one car driving 2 or 3 people to the same good job located in the suburbs. An undisrupted car ride will give them more time to not be stressed out- and at the mercy of so many variables beyond their control. The transportation cooperative has the potential to also provide more opportunities for people to get jobs not located on bus routes.

The landlord canvasser and negotiator will develop a systemic approach in influencing landlords to accept rental assistance by leveraging the guaranteed monthly rental payments and third party (program) support in mitigating tenant issues. And creating a database with geographic mapping abilities to try and accommodate (and spread out) anticipated exiting incarcerated populations. This team will also work with rental assistance service providers to provide shared information (gathered from canvassing) of practices that will enable them to expand their 'felony friendly' landlord network. Thus making the whole community more accepting.

The last six months of the program will focus on fulfilling the individual transition plans. They will also aggressively look for job opportunities, and be provided with a reference letter for general career advancement purposes. The 'overall' hope is that the community will be more thriving and welcoming to all its members actually living in it- with a grassroots and self-sustaining infrastructure to continue nurturing it.

Chapter Eight

Hobo Jungle
As performed by the Band

Let's get fundamental for a minute. The 'exploration and settling' of this land was done by Europeans from nations that were not dominating worldly affairs when they began. They had been on the 'other' side of the domination chain. So the world in itself was entering a whole new realm of exploitation, and the subsequent colonization carried out the art of exploitation to unimaginable levels (or attainable) prior to the 'encounter' and trans Atlantic slave trade.

The 'folks' that did the actual heavy lifting (or traveled the grueling two to three month voyage across the Atlantic and worked the land) were not sitting on thrones reaping in ill-gotten gains in the name of some crown. They were 'commoners'- who had been subject to pittance, and their subsistence was based on the temperament of their 'rulers.' So it is all the more baffling to consider how folks that were once subjected to harsh conditions caused by exploitation would later carry out such similar, and even more inhumane, practices.

The likelihood of surviving the trip was 'unknown' in itself- as well as the opportunities that existed on this side of the Atlantic. Many of the first English settlers were fleeing economic conditions of land redistribution (removal) or harsh conditions due to their religious beliefs (persecution). And when they said 'good bye' to their family before crossing the pond- they were 'really' saying good bye- knowing they would probably never reunite again.

And how about the 'African' slaves--- not only were they 'stripped' from their homelands- they were also stripped of any human rights as they were forced onto ships against their will … knowing they would never see their families again- imagine that 'goodbye.' Is it possible, for us so accustomed to the comfort and 'ease' of modern travel, to conceptualize how monumental the European encounter was in relation to kin and cultural preservation- or 'family' values? The Europeans and Africans were physically separated from their families and homelands- while the Native families and their homelands were purposely destroyed and seized by the 'powers that be.' So what exactly are we discussing in 'current' debates romanticizing the good old days of 'family' values?

I recently shed tears that did not belong to me (per se)- in discovering how persistence has allowed many Indian Nations in North America to 'win' back rights to their indigenous lands. The progression of how sovereignty is understood and practiced in this country is long over due, and illuminates how 'misguided' and thoughtless this country was in its infancy. I also have this tendency to be a 'romantic'- or really hope that all is not as bad as it appears.

It is easy to become disgusted and saddened when one really devours 'American' history at its core. I have inundated myself with various works of fiction and non-fiction from different viewpoints in relation to the 'European' encounter on the American continents. One 'constant' that ought to not be taken lightly is that 'tribal' warfare- or conflict- existed but the motivation of 'greed' did not.

Greed dominating practices (like acquiring gold or personal wealth) introduces a whole new can of worms into how individuals are allowed to live- because it imposes the notion of 'superiority'- which is not a basic element of survival. The 'reason' I shed tears over our government's relationship with indigenous populations is because rights are finally being established that respect self-sufficiency. This is a far cry from the 'government' practices of genocide and land removals in the past.

There is no way back to the 'way of life' prior to European invasion, but at the very least we are acknowledging and taking responsibility for the disruption. The 'pride' I feel in this progress is not on our government's behalf, but on behalf of the non-violent and vigilant actions of the Indian Nations- although their way of life (and land) was completely ransacked- they remain peaceful (not docile or dependent), because their cultural beliefs and practices have not been diminished despite thousands of attempts to do otherwise. I am moved by the fact that 'greed' has never 'appeared' to be a motivating factor in a their dealings with Europeans- and later with the U.S. government. They have set an example that so many can learn from.

I fantasize that the initial encounters among the people were more humane and cooperative than history demonstrates. That is, I imagine ferocious little wooden ships occupied with just as strong willed and tired people- whether coming from Europe or Africa- being met by peaceful and subsisting people. There was no 'initial' reason for colonization or conflict amongst the encountering peoples- it was the same system that influences injustice today that most surely played a role in the vast injustices created then.

It was the system that infused 'race' into a caste labor system. 'Rich' whites overseeing the exploitation of labor performed by 'poor' white and all non-white populations. I seek intellectual comfort in imagining that at least some of the folks, both practicing and witnessing the barbaric methods of genocide and slavery, were disgusted by such savagery- but were subject to adhering to such practices because of their positions in the system.

I can at least 'draw on' the amicable relationships described between early European traders and trappers with indigenous people to know that some peace existed- as well as the early white abolitionists speaking out against slavery. And stories of slaves fleeing to Indian Nations to live as 'free' people. But those stories are buried under the narratives of 'conflict'- almost as if an attempt has been made to establish some sort of long held division of humanity based on race.

Racism is a socially constructed idea- that manifested into an ideology to establish a caste system for labor-upon the European 'encounter' on the American continents. So it is very fundamental and crucial for people to understand that yes, the practice of slavery and ideas of racial superiority existed 'pre' colonial era; but not in conjunction or together as a means for a ruling power to extract wealth from labor and the acquisition of land (I have no shame in being repetitive on this point).

Aside from the politically motivated social progress made in this country- I've come to adore one of its economically motivated projects- the railroad. Yes, it occurred on the heels of the Civil War, and employed oppressive tactics on the Chinese laborers (or people) commissioned to complete the project- while destroying the ecological and hunting grounds for indigenous people. But it also developed a 'new' motivating interest for transportation that focused on the 'non labor' related movement of passengers.

The opportunity for 'people' to move about this land in relative comfort and economic ease was completely new- and was commissioned by both the government and private business interests. The completion of the intercontinental railroad is a remarkable time to consider in human history- simply because the 'idea' of visiting someone many miles away was made feasible. We must not discount the fact that the more 'adventurous' (or less financially able) could also hop on a moving car and move about the land for free- though eventually illegal.

The actual 'movement' of people is most impressive. A trip from New York to San Francisco was reduced, from the 'expensive' weeks at sea or the 'strenuous' months by wagon, to less than four days by rail. And the ability to 'convene' various meetings of the minds was no doubt a positive consequence of this development. This demonstrates a 'ruling' authority that was motivated beyond the 'old world' paradigm of pure greed, because it also embodied a sense of the 'for the people by the people' idealism.

We have further progressed in transportation methods that make a trip to the other side of the world be a matter of 'hours' instead of months- and intercontinental travel in the United States is even shorter. Seriously, one ought to be truly humbled when realizing the 'time' we are living in. Consider the longstanding modes of travel prior to the 16th and 17th centuries- there was nothing but human or animal powered vessels (whether by land or water) that were very dependent on the wind and weather.

All sorts of populations have relocated and traveled all over the world- again, creating the ability for even more various meeting of the minds- not to mention the 'click of a mouse' speed to send correspondence. So why are so many well-intentioned people left with allowing injustice to continue? Why do we permit the 'ideas' of fear and conflict to limit our practices of compassionate humanity?

I reside in a 'developed and affluent' society that allows homelessness to exist right in front of its face- I became disenchanted with the occupy movement on United States soil, because I truly wonder why people- who allow such an injustice like homelessness to occur in its own backyard- would suddenly care about different forms of injustice?

But, then again, I do think individual introspection can bring about better collective action. And that may be the remedy necessary for this fast paced traveling and communicating society. Think of the workers 'rights' movement in this country- and the creation of laws to determine proper hours and conditions of labor that nearly every employed person benefits. These were concepts that became a reality. Today we spend time determining a 'hostile' work environment, and fail to realize how 'privileged' we all are to be able to do so.

My great-great grandmother- who fled Missouri in her youth because of the 'life threatening' hostility of Southern sympathizers (Civil War era)- eventually married and had children after the war, then lost her husband and daughter to illness- causing her to take on the 'business' affairs for the family, eventually moving herself and remaining three children to a town with good college and employment opportunities- only to have the college and factory in the town burn down- which led them back to the family farm- a safety net of subsistence unknown (and unavailable) to most of us in the 21st century.

Not that farm life is anything 'easy' or stable- but it provides opportunities to put food on the table. In the middle of the 19th century, there was no safety net for people other than 'people.'   Many walks of life were actually starving and subject to financial instability in ways we take for granted today.

The workers 'rights' (late 19th century) and the civil 'rights' (mid 20th century) movements in this country demonstrate the ongoing fight 'people' have engaged in to be treated fairly by ruling authorities. The actual 'government' of this country was not established until the 18th century- and was nearly destroyed, not even 100 years after its inception, as it ended the practice of slavery- the practice of claiming human 'ownership' over other humans.

Slavery, in this country, was and is an economic labor tactic rooted in racism. The workers and civil rights movements would not have existed without the abolition of slavery. Thus, the worker and civil rights movements were struggles to move 'with' the foundation of this country while establishing fair and humane practices for future generations. The fact that the basic tenets of participating in a democracy were unable to legally coalesce until the mid 20th century- that is, all women and communities of color were finally able to cast their votes in a government 'for the people by the people' indicates that the fight is not (and has never been) over.

So many lives were lost in these former peoples movements in order to bring about lasting change- and I hope those of us living today don't vacate these interconnected and painstaking efforts because of our vanity. We allow our personalities to divide us, which is counterintuitive to the benign power 'hardship' has in uniting us.

Studying abroad, spending every Christmas in Tahiti, or traveling for employment reasons are 'things' that many people have done since I was born (although I have done none of them myself... aside from homelessness related 'business' I traveled to Oakland CA in 2006, Culver City CA in 2007 and Chicago IL in 2009). Between these 'types' of reasons (and war) to travel- the overall population mixture has changed both in this country and around the world.

142

We must also consider that the various inter-racial breeding between people has created even more 'compositions' of human 'ethnic' and 'racial' offspring to the already convoluted classification system. There are two distinct metaphor theories of the United States being either a "melting pot" or a "tossed salad" – the former being a blended culture mixture of the parts and the latter being an unblended culture mixture. Do we really care? What purpose do such distinctions of racial and ethnic classifications serve? (I understand the practical reasons, but 'overall'- who is benefiting from maintaining this system?).

For all I know, the family trail that I can't trace back could be an assortment of Native or African American blood- and my 'traceable' ancestors may have 'mixed' offspring that I don't even know about. What difference would it make on me today? Skin 'tone' is a surface reality that should not determine the opportunities one is offered. Neither should religious beliefs- the persecution of it is a reason that continues to attract different people to this land today. A person's individual belief on 'how or why' they exist in this world should have no bearing on how they are treated- or is not a basis for discrimination.

My mother's family toured Europe by Volkswagen camper bus in the 1960's. They relied on 'parks' and other public accommodations for their travels- not Ritz Carlton's or other five star hotels. My first trip to the Virgin Islands utilized a campground facility (I was 2-years-old)- a couple months ago, over 20 members of my family (pretty much the same contingency as the first trip) stayed at such a swanky place I'm embarrassed to admit it. Or not embarrassed, but amazed in the difference of lodging choices today as opposed to 30 years ago. The hotels and commercial enterprises so common in various 'hotspots' around the world is an extremely 'modern' industry- and perhaps a 'good' sign since vacation travel is designed and pursued in the interest 'relaxation' instead of war.

The travel evolution of it in the 20th century certainly brought a lot of people in contact with one another from around the world- and most likely taught people that they are not that 'different'- or at least established concrete evidence that the 'people' aren't necessarily at odds with one another- ruling authorities choose conflict, not people. I've heard that the most contested 'religious' area in Israel is peacefully respected and visited by its distinct Muslim, Jewish and Christian followers. So again, people really don't have intrinsic 'conflict' wired in them- all the hoopla and drama surrounding conflict is an off-shoot of systemic battles, of which creates the conditions that people are subject to live within and around.

Therefore, I think it is time for everyone, relishing in 21st century creature comforts, to really 'think' about how we got to where we are today- and begin collectively fighting and sacrificing for 'things' of substance- or rights that future generations can live with. People are 'concerned' about others (I hope)- and engage in all sorts of charity or fundraising drives for lord knows how many 'causes.' That's great- but do we really want our imprint in history to be one of individual causes?

I realize there is an exorbitant amount of health and environmental 'issues' that deserve attention, but we ought to pick up where our predecessors left off. A human 'rights' movement is the fundamental successor to the worker and civil rights movements. Establishing a 'baseline' for human 'rights' is essential, not only for ensuring every person is entitled to safe 'shelter' (and by that I mean a literal shelter, not the 'modern' institution of it); and is also a vital step in resolving the deeply entrenched conceptualism of racism- because racism (as disastrous and unfounded as it is) is the concept that transformed the 'idea' of labor from being an imposed institution benefiting very few to one that now has opportunities to benefit many.

Shall we be remembered as a generation that allowed the conditions of poverty and homelessness to exist and exacerbate while we all went into debt buying shit for ourselves? Are we comfortable knowing that we have the highest incarcerated population in the world- and that far too many of these people are serving time for 'non-violent' crimes and are over represented by communities of color? There is already attention and resources being directed to some of these socioeconomic issues by the government, universities, religious institutions, private foundations, individual donors, 'concerned' citizens and a whole world of dedicated 'on the ground' people engaging in the fight for justice- so the 'missing' entity is really the collective will of the 'people.'

We (as in the benefactors of a society with established worker and civil 'rights') are relatively 'comfortable' enough in obtaining 'our' survival needs, and ought to make sure everyone else is able to meet theirs- especially those whose paths to meeting them are being infringed upon due to 'our' comfort.

We owe future generations the attainment of equality. I really do think that our founding fathers hoped for such human progress- otherwise why would they 'open' such a revolutionary document to the founding of this country declaring such? As if it wasn't scrutinized enough before being adapted for someone to have said, "Hey, buddy, that sentence about 'all men are created equal' kind of contradicts our slavery and 'domestication' of Native population practices..."

It is very difficult to make a 'concept' a reality. And economic, social and political progressions are made in every generation- so we ought to decide what ours will be. I will not be satisfied as just a 'cause' generation- we need to continue the evolution of establishing 'rights.'

And pursuing fundamental human rights may also settle the ongoing dispute of 'who' has a right to get married- a 'privilege' that in its current form did not turn out all warm and fuzzy for me (and around 50% of other married couples)- so what are we collectively holding onto? The question really becomes how 'comfortable' is your sleep (or conscience) knowing that our way of life allows so many people to live without the 'right' to have a comfortable sleep- an 'issue' that does not necessarily require more 'money' to solve- just a comprehensive shift in our collective priorities.

Think about it, when did 'homelessness' become a sign of weakness rather than a badge of honor? And why are the 'afflicted'- or surviving- treated as criminals and trespassers instead of as heroes and warriors? I have a 'sense' and understanding of when it became a public 'nuisance' issue in this modern era, and the 'narrative' and other 'facts' that are attached to it- as well as the 'actual' conditions. But reverting to 'fundamentals'...aren't the early revered European 'settlers and explorers' of this land its original homeless population?

And weren't they all of 'white' decent? We hardly 'ever' consider 'those' pioneers to be criminals or trespassers. Is that because of anything other than our collective understanding of the issue? And 'public' understanding seems to always be swayed by propaganda. Are we all not smarter than that? The whole world is feeling the pinch of injustice from those holding the power of wealth- and we ought to demand that everyone is to be treated as human with equal rights.

The 'Occupy Wall Street' movement is almost 'cute' because it is easy to connect it to many people- but in reality, it is just another 'cause' to throw attention at- and I cannot conceptualize how it will resolve societal injustice as it is being carried out on U.S. soil. The money and power residing in Wall Street would not exist if not for the racist economy extracted on the backs of those who faced genocide and slavery- so we ought to focus on those roots.

Addressing the conditions in which our society allows homelessness to exist is a practical first step, because if done thoroughly- it will lead to establishing human rights. That is, an overall objective in ending homelessness should focus on making access to suitable housing a human right. This requires a different mobilization effort than fending off the banks from foreclosing on individual household homes- while an admirable task- it still encompasses the individualism methodology that does not create better 'rights' and conditions for everyone.

The evolution of 'rights' will decrease the 'causes' related to poverty because more people will have access to employment and housing- which will produce a much healthier and stable (cost effective) society. It also continues the struggle to conceptualize into reality the notion our founding fathers highly regarded in believing that 'all men are created equal.'

I really do believe in my heart of hearts that people care about other people and are willing to make sacrifices in order to have a more just society, but the growth and presence of homelessness- as well as the knowledge of our incarcerated population- 'causes' me to believe otherwise. Moving on collectively and comprehensively from such injustice requires a vigorous analysis of the concept of racism and how it has shaped our society. We, as in the people, have the power to care for people- regardless of money or corporate interests- so channeling our efforts into a more concrete battle of establishing rights for people, instead of against the abstract notion of greed against institutions, will empower and improve our collective strength within the 'system.'

Because I believe, in the case of humanity, that racism is 'curable'- whereas greed is not.
Homelessness, in the 21st century United States of America, is a grave discomfort caused by greed, and curable by the collective will of the people- and we need to eradicate it in this country so that humanity can move forward together- and away from the conditions of poverty.

Cue in "Dark End of the Street"

-As performed by James Carr

Niece and Nephew (2012)

Me, Bro & Sis (2007)

Dad, Me & Alaskan Pipeline (2002)

My first personal desktop computer (1998)

Family photo taken for church directory and used as Christmas card (1991)

Goofy picture dad took while on vacation in Colorado. Although it was a 'working' vacation for him- and for her too, when you think about it (1984)

My dad's youngest bro is petting Brutus in front. Back row starting from left: Dad's other bro, Dad's mother, Dad's little sis, himself (1960's)

Maternal grandparents 'courting' while in college (1940's)

Great grandmother and grandfather (Maternal grandfather's parents) enjoying time at the family cabin they built in the 1930's (1970's)

Maternal great grandmother with my 3x great grandfather (her grandfather) who was a farmer in Wisconsin (1893)

My great-great grandmother referenced in book- who fled Missouri
in her youth because of the 'life threatening' hostility of Southern
sympathizers (Civil War era). My pictured great-great grandfather
must have passed away shortly after this photo was taken.

156

My father being held by his father (1940)

3x great grandfather- Minneapolis lumber 'baron' that probably
traveled by covered wagon, with his whole family, from Maine to
Minnesota in the mid 19th century (Photo credit to the Minnesota
Historical Society, taken late 19th century)

Me & Rocky- the original 'Lhasa' in my life (R.I.P. to the noble beast, 1991 – 2006)

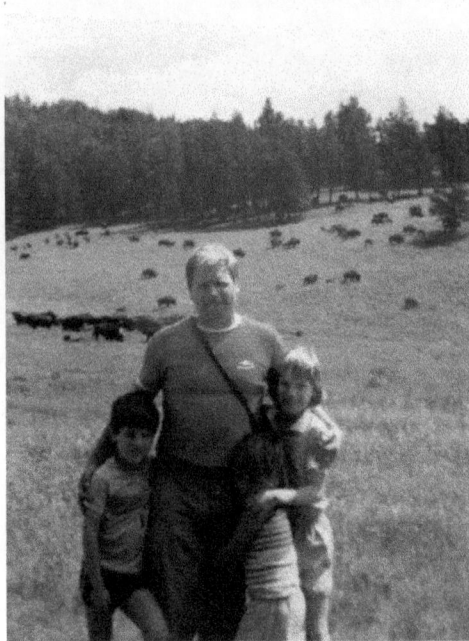

Picture mom took of us posing with buffalo in South Dakota

Words I would have put somewhere- since I don't have some large media conglomerate or famous person to advertise for me...

I've been bamboozled, betrayed, insulted, broke and broken down! But guess what, this book isn't about my private life journey of struggles. I share what I think is conducive for the task at hand. I try to stay positive. I realize people are well intentioned when they say 'just remember someone always has it worse than you' when I'm feeling down—you know what I want say (but I politely thank them for the reminder since it is said so often)...

160

We are all in this thing called life together, so if I can't feel down without having to 'remember' someone's always got it worse than I do (which actually makes ME feel worse, not better) than leave me alone! No more have and have not comparisons to cure temporary blues- let's make sure we all are better. I don't see the logic in lifting our individual spirits at the expense of someone else's misfortune. We all have our personal 'good' days and 'bad' days, and we need them so that we can be stronger and appreciate what we do have. And THAT will help us make sure the quality of life is more equal for everyone- instead of being fake walking contradictions of ourselves.

How do you sleep at night?